THE BOOK OF ART is designed as an introduction to the visual arts: painting, drawing and sculpture. It provides a comprehensive survey, in ten volumes, of one of the most creative aspects of human effort, especially organized for the reader who does not have an extensive knowledge of the history of art.

Textual material prepared by experts in each school of art presents a detailed background of information. But, since art must be seen to be understood and appreciated, the essence of each volume lies in the color plates and the large number of black-and-white illustrations.

The first volume discusses the origins of the visual arts in the western world. The following five volumes are devoted to national schools of painting, extending roughly from the early Renaissance up to the mid-19th century. The two succeeding volumes cut across national divisions and deal first with the Impressionists and Post-Impressionists and then with 20th-century art. The ninth volume deals with the rich art of China and Japan.

The final volume, *How to Look at Art*, is designed to aid the reader in developing an appreciative understanding of the entire field of art. It discusses art of all schools and periods, with relevant illustrations, both in color and black-and-white, throughout the text. The same volume concludes with an illustrated glossary of art terms and a comprehensive index covering all ten volumes.

THE BOOK OF ART

A Pictorial Encyclopedia of Painting, Drawing, and Sculpture

VOLUME 3

FLEMISH AND DUTCH ART

THE BOOK OF ART
A Pictorial Encyclopedia of Painting, Drawing, and Sculpture

FLEMISH AND DUTCH ART

Edited, with an Introduction, by

Professor A. M. Hammacher

Former Director, Rijksmuseum Kröller-Müller, Otterlo

and

Dr. R. Hammacher Vandenbrande

Boymans-van Beuningen Museum, Rotterdam

Grolier
INCORPORATED

NEW YORK   MONTREAL   MEXICO CITY   SYDNEY

HOW TO USE THIS BOOK

To obtain the maximum information and interest from this series it is necessary to understand its basic plan. With the exception of the first volume and the last two volumes, which are more general in their scope, each of the other seven volumes is arranged as follows:

First, a historical Introduction sets out the main lines of development within the school or period, with special reference to the major artists and the major works of art.

This is followed by a biographical section outlining the life and work of every major artist and important minor artists. The Biographies run in alphabetical order according to the name by which each artist is most generally known, whether it be surname, or Christian name (as for example LEONARDO da Vinci), or nickname (as TINTORETTO). With each biography is given a cross-reference to the page or pages on which he is represented in the plates sections which follow; a monochrome reproduction of one or more of his other works; and (where possible) a self-portrait or portrait of the artist and a specimen of his signature.

Next follow the sections of Color Plates, Drawings, and Sculpture. Each of these sections is arranged in chronological order according to the date of the artist's birth, though in a few cases minor adjustments to this order have been made for the sake of comparison or design. To illustrate painting techniques, particularly of frescoes and large easel paintings, some color plates show a detail rather than the whole work; but the use of such a detail is indicated in the caption, and a monochrome illustration of the whole work is normally given with the artist's biography; in such cases the size given in the caption refers to the whole painting. The location of every work of art is included in its caption. Every effort has been made to include also the size, medium, and date of each work represented in the plates, though this has not always been possible since not every museum has such information available for all the items in its collection. The reader will also appreciate that the precise dating of many works of art is the subject of scholarly controversy; however, no dates have been included here unless they have the authority of qualified experts and art historians.

A final section, entitled Influences and Developments, rounds off the period by drawing together the main ideas and characteristics of schools and styles, and by exploring the internal and external influences that have made their impact on the development of the arts during the period concerned.

A list of basic reference books for further reading appears on page 16. Books containing material of special interest concerning an individual artist are listed at the end of the relevant biography.

To avoid repetitive explanation of basic technical terms such as *genre, chiaroscuro, baroque,* etc., an illustrated Glossary is provided in the volume entitled *How to Look at Art.* Also in that volume is an Index listing every artist mentioned throughout the series.

Taken as a whole, the series thus provides a comprehensive, carefully integrated, and highly informative survey of the achievement and significance of Western Art from its origins to the present day.

NOTE.—The terminal dates in the titles of some of the volumes are inevitably approximate. One volume will sometimes overlap with another. Some artists mentioned under French Art, for example, are also represented under the Impressionists, and the Post-Impressionists merge imperceptibly with the Moderns. In the ever-continuous process of Art it is difficult to contain schools or periods within precise boundaries.

Copyright (©) 1965 by Grolier Incorporated
First published 1965. Second Impression 1966. Third Impression 1967. Fourth Impression 1967.
Library of Congress Catalog Card Number: 65-10350

Designed and produced by George Rainbird Ltd., London
PRINTED IN ITALY by Amilcare Pizzi S.p.A., Milan

Contents

LIST OF COLOR PLATES

ACKNOWLEDGMENTS

The publishers and producers wish to express their gratitude to all the museums, art galleries, collectors, photographers, and agencies who have courteously assisted them in obtaining the material for the illustrations reproduced in this volume. They would especially like to thank the following:

Albertina, Vienna
Alte Pinakothek, Munich
Ampliaciones y Reproducciones Mas, Barcelona
The Wellington Museum, Apsley House, London
Archives Centrales Iconographiques d'Art National, Brussels
The Ashmolean Museum, Oxford, England
Association des Artistes Professionels de Belgique, Brussels

L'Autorisation de la Commission de l'Assistance Publique, Bruges
Paul L. van Bessem, Amsterdam
Bibliothèque Nationale, Paris
Bibliothèque Royale de Belgique, Brussels
Paul Bijtebier, Brussels
Joachim Blauel, Munich
The Trustees of the British Museum, London
Ets. J. E. Bulloz, Paris
Caisse Nationale des Monuments Historiques, Paris
Centraal Museum der Gemeente, Utrecht
The Governing Body, Christ Church College, Oxford
Rex A. L. Cohen, London

2

3

ABBREVIATIONS

attrib.	attributed, attribution
et al.	and elsewhere
in.	inches
St.	Saint (English and German)
St. or Ste.	Saint (French)
S.	Saint (Italian and Spanish)
B-A.	Beaux-Arts
B.M.	British Museum, London
Bibl. Nat.	Bibliothèque Nationale
Cath.	Cathedral
Coll.	Collection
Fitzwm.	Fitzwilliam Museum, Cambridge, England
Gal.	Galerie
Gall.	Gallery, Galleria
Gemäldegal.	Gemäldegalerie
Inst.	Institute, Institut
Kunsthist.	Kunsthistorisches
Kunstsamm.	Kunstsammlung
Kunstinst.	Kunstinstitut
Mus.	Musée, Museen, Museo, Museum
Nationalmus.	Nationalmuseum
Nat.	National, Nationale
Naz.	Nazionale
N.G.	National Gallery, London
	National Gallery of Art, Washington, D. C.
	Nasjonalgalleriet, Oslo
	National Gallery of Scotland, Edinburgh
N.P.G.	National Portrait Gallery, London
Pal.	Palace, Palazzo
Pin.	Pinacoteca, Pinacothèque, Pinakothek
Royal Coll.	Royal Collection, England
Soc.	Society

Introduction

Flemish and Dutch Art

The title "Flemish and Dutch Art" evokes a vision of still-life studies and kitchen scenes, brown-green landscapes, genre paintings, dignified groups of 17th-century families and guilds, representations of bourgeois ladies and gentlemen, and engaging portraits of pipesmokers and topers. It conjures up Jan van Eyck and his aristocratic environment, Hans Memling and the city of Bruges, Rubens in Antwerp, and Rembrandt in Amsterdam. But although the art of the Netherlands is generally regarded as primarily an art of painting, the illustrations in the following pages show that it is also well represented in the fields of drawing and sculpture. In particular, the relatively large number of drawings included in this volume not only illustrates the extraordinary richness, variety, and directness of Flemish and Dutch draftsmanship but also provides a vivid insight into the lives of ordinary people.

The beginnings of art in the Netherlands

This is no place to describe in detail the political processes by which the small communities of the Middle Ages—the cities, bishoprics, and counties—became the two larger units of the Republic of the United Netherlands (the predecessor of the modern kingdom), and the Spanish Netherlands, which underwent Austrian rule and eventually gained independence as the kingdom of Belgium. The art of painting did not make its appearance as the merely accidental achievement of a number of highly gifted individuals. Long before its first flowering in the late 14th and 15th centuries, the life of the spirit had shown itself in a richly developed literature. The passionate lyricism of "Sister Hadewych," mystic and poetess of Antwerp, who died in about 1270, showed in its visionary fervor and command of language the existence of an exceptional culture, in which women were evidently important as creative artists. Van Maerlant and Ruysbroeck were not only scholars with a tendency to mysticism but also progressive thinkers. Polyphonic music was first developed in the Netherlands in the 15th century, and, as in Italy, was used in secular as well as religious music. Composers such as Obrecht, Ockeghem, des Pres, Dufay, and Lassus became the dominant influence on 15th-century European music. Flemish painting was cradled in this culture of new developments.

Manuscript illumination

In the 13th century manuscript illuminators were already freeing themselves from the shackles of medievalism, and seeking, partly influenced by English artists, to give shape to the growing interest in nature and human concerns. Flanders, with Utrecht and Gelderland, produced masters in this field. They were distinguished from French and Italian miniaturists by a keen perception, not so much of what was beautiful in itself, but of the realities of everyday life. They were the precursors of Hieronymus Bosch and Pieter Bruegel the Elder. Their vigorous art extended well into the 15th century, showing signs of degeneration only in the 16th.

The crafts of medieval times

The political unrest among the numerous minor states of the pre-Reformation era appears to have been no obstacle to uniformity of style. Both the lesser bourgeoisie and the rich merchants, who were also civic dignitaries, demanded objects of art. Carpets were woven; silver was molded and chased into chains and maces for burgomasters, chalices and crowns for statues of the Virgin; furniture was carved and stained glass windows were designed and constructed. Skilled journeymen prepared the work which their masters completed with the utmost refinement.

Art in the court

This artistic activity was based on the town and the small agricultural communities which formed around cloister and castle. Only the Burgundian court commissioned objects of art for its own delight and glorification, after the manner of aristocrats. The cities of the North developed later than those of the South; although by the 15th century the church was no longer the chief patron of the arts in the South, it still influenced life at the court of Burgundy. A page from an illuminated manuscript of the second half of the 15th century illustrates this well. The page represents Philip the Good hearing High Mass in the court chapel, and it is a complete epitome of contemporary Burgundian life. The duke is seen kneeling under a canopy beside the altar in a little chapel; against a background of worshipping courtiers the central figures are the singing monks and the celebrant at the altar. Perspective is far less developed than in Italy, where the young Masaccio, in Renaissance Florence a quarter of a century earlier, had found the secret of unifying space and form. The page, with its partly Gothic arrangement of the folds of the garments, its flat, bright colors, and the absence of distinct lighting, shows the liturgical act at a particular moment, and depicts the individual, not the type. The style is bourgeois rather than aristocratic; despite the religious theme, the painter shows a restrained humor in his vivid perception of the wooden features of the participants. He is far removed from the imposing serenity which Masaccio expressed in his men and women drawn from the streets of Florence; far, too, from the graceful motions of Masolino's figures.

Philip the Bold was a skilled warrior and an accomplished statesman. Both at home and on his many journeys with his large train of courtiers he loved to surround himself with beautiful things—tapestries, gorgeous cloths, jewels, and magnificent books. In his day, not only the citizenry and the church, but also the court were the patrons of a highly developed art, both religious and secular. Artists and craftsmen, few in number but much in demand, were of necessity itinerant, and the dissemination of ideas which resulted from their journeys produced a style in which unity and diversity were wedded. The illumination and illustration of books was an important activity that had begun long before the great school of the van Eycks gained ascendancy and influenced even Italy. The best of the illustrators wandered through Europe, traveling from commission to commission, their origin always apparent in their work. The Maelwaels, natives of Nijmegen, worked at Dijon and Paris and were related to the three de Limbourg brothers. These brothers, between 1411 and 1416, illustrated a breviary, the famous *Tres Riches Heures*, for the Duke of Berri. This exquisite work was the flower of years of slow development.

Sculptors

Sculptors at this time were of course even more dependent on the church than other artists. Much less is known of their workshops and methods than of those of the illuminators. It is difficult to distinguish personal styles, but here too the anonymous and collective art of the Middle Ages was giving way to individuality. Compared with their great French models, the cathedrals of Utrecht, 's Hertogenbosch, and Brussels have a comfortably provincial character. The church of Halle (p. 257) in Belgium has impressive figures of apostles that date from the beginning of the 15th century. The bishopric of Utrecht, whose illuminators offered at one time such competition to those of Bruges that the magistrates of the latter city forbade the importation of their work, also had two powerful sculptors, Adriaen van Wesel and the Master of Joachim and Anna. There was a controlled yet profound spirituality in the work of the Gothic sculptors, that resembles the unostentatious but passionate piety in the mystical literature of the late 13th century.

Van Wesel's angel-musicians in his relief-like altar panels (p. 260) are a reminder of the joy that was undoubtedly aroused by the new polyphony of the 15th century. He produced unaided the carving for the altar of 's Hertogenbosch Cathedral; the panels of the altar-piece were painted by no less an artist than Hieronymus Bosch. In *The Meeting of Joachim and Anna* (p. 262), the work of an anonymous master, as in van Wesel's suggestion of rapturous attention to the music-making angels, can be seen both the expression of an inner life of profound devotion and the clear observation of real and living human beings. This observation of actual men and women is clear evidence of the new spirit of the time and of the peculiar contribution made to it by the artists of the Netherlands. By its representation of space and the coloring of the carved figures, sculpture greatly affected painting. The painters responded to the stimulus of three-dimensional art and of carving in relief. They consciously imitated the sculptors, and their perception of the human form was obviously influenced by sculptured figures. Many carved altarpieces show an abundance of gold and other colors, while in painting sculpture is imitated in a subdued grisaille. The two arts do not merely approach one another; they come into close contact.

Claus Sluter

The dominating figure in Dutch sculpture of this time was Claus Sluter of Haarlem. Though his art may not be closely associated with any particular school or workshop, he may have had some affiliations with German sculpture of the Naumberg style. It is certain that when, from 1398 on, he worked at Dijon for Philip the Bold, Duke of Burgundy, Sluter deflected Gothic sculpture into a new channel. The Chartreuse de Champmol near Dijon, where Sluter succeeded Jean de Marville, became an important site for the new sculpture. The Old Testament prophets of *The Well of Moses* (p. 259) may seem reminiscent of the sculptures decorating cathedrals, but Sluter has made them almost autonomous figures, structurally united only in that they constitute a group and are no longer subservient to architecture.

The striking features of the group of *The Well of Moses* are its dramatic force and the powerfully "commonplace" character of the tormented prophets. If one remembers that they were originally colored, they are reminiscent of Masaccio's painted figures which were undoubtedly influenced by sculpture, and which exhibit a similar solemn and fierce humanity; not figures of

some abstract hereafter, but men of the artist's own city. That other Florentine, Donatello, with a more ancient background than Sluter's, and a different society, achieved the same accent on the typical life of the people. North and South confronted the same problem, posed by the awakening from the Gothic dream to the reality of the human situation. Their answer was to depict man heroically, dignified spiritually, but unmistakably human.

Two very different attitudes to death are to be found in Sluter's work. One may be seen in the tomb of Philip the Bold, with its procession of mourners in their enveloping sculptured draperies; a theatrical scene of impressive grandeur in which the simplicity of the Christian ideas of redemption and release from earthly cares is lost. More genuinely moving is Sluter's most beautiful work—the head of Christ (p. 258), from a crucifix which was originally part of *The Well of Moses*, but was detached from it in the 18th century. It lacks not only the repressed and pathetic expression of the German late-Gothic Christs, but also the sublime, self-restrained spirituality of the French. The crown of thorns, the hair, and the beard are close to the terrible last death-struggle; only in the face is there aloofness and dignity.

With the growing power of the Burgundian court, German influence tended to decline and the cultural ascendancy of the French to assert itself. The art of Dijon, however, displays many Flemish characteristics. Sluter's work there was continued by his nephew Claus de Werve, a native of Hattem in the Northern Netherlands, as well as by French and even Spanish craftsmen.

Much sculptural work was done in Flanders after Sluter, both by native artists and by visitors from abroad, and important work was produced in the Baroque style in the 17th century, but Sluter's unique sense of form was never again attained. He died at the beginning of the 15th century, which saw the start of the chain of events which was to lead to the final political separation of the North and South Netherlands into Holland in the North and the Roman Catholic provinces in the South under the Spanish rule of Philip II. This century also saw the beginning of the tradition in painting which was to lead from Jan van Eyck, through Hieronymus Bosch, to Pieter Bruegel the Elder.

Jan van Eyck

Art historians have disputed the importance and even the existence of Hubert van Eyck, Jan's brother; it is now established that Hubert lived, and, in his own lifetime, was considered the greater artist. The use of oil paints, whose invention was once attributed to the van Eyck brothers, was well known before their day, as is proved by the paints used on statuary. However, Jan van Eyck raised the technique to a perfection that had great influence in Europe. He illustrates the high degree of general culture to which a Flemish artist of his day could aspire. He was sent on diplomatic missions, traveled in Spain and Portugal, and was a man of letters as well as a great painter. The special characteristics of his art were the powerful luminosity of his intense colors, and the vigor of his all-embracing, minutely detailed observation of reality. Although he did not equal the Italians' mastery of perspective, every facet of life shines so positively in his work that outward appearance and inward spirit form an indivisible unity.

With van Eyck's followers this objectivity, full of tension and radiance in the master's own work, became unemotional and flat. In a room full of portraits it is instantly obvious which are his; the smallest work is a miracle of absolute sympathy in which nothing is falsely embellished and nothing left indistinct. With almost scientific care he confers aesthetic distinction on the slightest detail. The famous *Portrait of Giovanni Arnolfini and his Wife* (p. 130), with the charming little dog at their feet and the mirror between them, contains the very essence of his skill as a painter. It still has a medieval atmosphere, showing middle-class life in a motionless instant of ritual. The bright light and the quiet shadows tie the transient moment to the unending passage of time.

Van Eyck's contemporaries and followers

Van Eyck's paintings were not the only beautiful works of art produced in his time. Robert Campin of Tournai, often identified with the Master of Flémalle, painted the Mérode altarpiece with its central *Annunciation* (p. 127). Campin coupled van Eyck's precision with a different kind of clarity; in him the all-pervading light which connects van Eyck's objects is lacking; his forms are more sculptural, more tangible. Hans Memling's earnest portraits (p. 137), warm and delicate as velvet, leave an impression of femininity and even of decadence when compared with those of the Hollander, Dieric Bouts (p. 134), with their compactness, strong vertical patterns, and severe stillness. Hugo van der Goes lets a personal emotionalism express itself in the visionary, wild, or grief-distorted faces of his subjects, seen for instance in *The Adoration of the Shepherds* (p. 135). Campin's pupil, Roger van der Weyden, introduces a new note after van Eyck's domination by his more stylized portrayal of life, less reticent expression of emotion, and the deliberate striving after beauty in his compositions. Among painters who followed his example is Geertgen tot Sint Jans, unlike the other a Northerner, who died toward the end of the century aged only 28. His limited output bears witness both to his great talent and to an exquisitely poetic mind, which shows itself in the mysterious light of the dark stable of *The Nativity*, and in the paradisal landscape of *St. John the Baptist in the Wilderness* (p. 140).

Hieronymus Bosch

In the work of Hieronymus Bosch the medieval spirit lived on in a special form. After van Eyck all the extravagances of the Romanesque style—monsters grimacing from gargoyles and choirstalls, devils leering from the margins of manuscripts, hideously distorted human souls being pitchforked into hell—seemed to have been exorcised from art. In Bosch this diabolic life returned in full force. He represents the world as a teeming anthill; his pictures resemble extended miniatures and must be read symbol by symbol. At a distance their effect is lost. Such titles as *The Garden of Delights*, *The Hay Cart*, and *The Temptation of St. Anthony* show that he relished the lewd and licentious world, but he was also a moralist, displaying the hold of the devil on human life. The element of fantasy in his work—the broken objects, insects, larvae, lustful and misshapen human beings, fruit and eggs endowed with limbs, deformed trees—give it an inexhaustible fascination. His style of painting is delicate and vividly graphic, his colors pure and transparent. The pictured moralizations, such as *The Ship of Fools* (p. 141), show his keen perception of the vivid imagery of popular speech, and his work as a whole is a rich mine for the modern psychoanalyst. Bosch had his precursors in the illuminators of manuscripts; he himself was the harbinger of Bruegel.

Quentin Massys, Bosch's longer-lived contemporary, was less fantastic. His portraits especially displayed the humanism of the time, while the atmosphere of Bruges still clung about his representation of his subjects.

Pieter Bruegel the Elder

In the 16th century the works of Pieter Bruegel the Elder are an epitome of an undermined and changing world. This was to be the age of Mannerism; the classical proportions and forms were losing their stability. The formulas produced by the rational spirit of the Renaissance became fluid, giving more opportunity for the exercise of the imagination. Even the increasing understanding of perspective sometimes resulted in its laws being carried to extremes. This century, which saw both the Reformation and the Counter-Reformation, was also a period of contrast between tradition and innovation in the arts, seen in the antithesis of classical and Baroque. In general the Protestantism of the Northern Netherlands was expressed in a controlled Baroque style, while the true and more exuberant Baroque flourished in the South, where it was fostered by the Jesuits, the new Catholic militia, as the triumphant expression in painting and architecture of the Church's claims.

Bruegel, who died rather young, experienced much of the unrest and hardship of his times, in Antwerp, Brussels, and on his travels in Italy and Sicily. He knew religious persecution, iconoclasm, famine, plague, and war. Nothing in his work has a separate existence; his human figures are types rather than individuals, and in his own way he unites the landscape with man's activities and with the seasons. Like Bosch he felt keenly the relationships between things, and knew the tragedy and pain inherent in life itself. Also like Bosch, he depicted the wisdom contained in popular proverbs and speech (p. 149); he collected and analyzed the games of children and the pastimes of adults. His drolleries continued the moralizing habit of the Middle Ages, showing a deep love of his country and its people.

Bruegel's work impresses because of his powerful, comprehensive vision, which simplifies and stylizes reality to accord with his consciousness of the universal. Never occupying itself solely with the individual, his warmly observant mind accentuated the general aspects of his subjects. Just as van Gogh's portrait of the wife of the postman Roulin has been given the title *Berceuse* and has become the archetype of the motherly housewife, so Bruegel's pictures portray *the* countryman, *the* dancer, *the* lover.

Baroque art in Belgium

In the Baroque art of the Southern Netherlands this humanism underwent a profound change. Under the viceregent Isabella, daughter of Philip II, the court of Brussels represented a solemn, formal element in a city where life in general was free and gay. Emigrants from France, often wealthy and important people, strengthened the French element in the language of the people. Convents and churches made religion a very practical part of daily life. The Flemings imbued their art with their own style, less elegant than the French, less stylized than the Italian, but full of life.

Rubens and the Flemish school

The central figure of the Flemish school, centered chiefly on Antwerp, was Rubens, who like van Eyck before him, was an important figure in public life. His skill and almost unlimited capacity for work earned him a European reputation in his own time and a continuing influence since. In his studio—so large that it has been called a factory—assistants and students helped him with his commissions. His themes were manifold—religious in *The Deposition*, ceremonial in *The Coronation of Maria de' Medici*, secular in *The Straw Hat* (p. 155), mythical in *Diana*, and rustic in *Landscape with Rainbow* (p. 156). Whatever his subject, his work bore the stamp of a great colorist, a master of complex composition, and a magnificent draftsman.

A more specialized painter, courtly and urbane—at times almost effeminate—was the portrait painter Anthony van Dyck, celebrated chiefly for his work at the English court of Charles I. In the same era, dominated by the Flemish Baroque style, Cornelis Floris represented the less exuberant tradition, with a clearly perceptible 16th-century background.

The difference between North and South

The importance of the division between the Protestant North and the Catholic South can be exaggerated. True, Rubens would have been out of place at Amsterdam or The Hague, and Jacob Jordaens, with his touch of Caravaggio's Italian style and his art rooted in the people of Antwerp, at Utrecht. Yet Adriaen van Ostade and Jan Steen are not so far removed from David Teniers or Adriaen Brouwer. Jacob van Campen, painter and architect of Amsterdam's Baroque Town Hall, was helped by masters from both Amsterdam and Antwerp. Jordaens decorated the stadtholders' palace, the Huis ten Bosch near The Hague. Van Campen created opportunities for Flemish sculptors; Artus Quellinus of Antwerp worked in Amsterdam for some 14 years on decorative sculpture for the Town Hall and organized the whole group of decorators. Hendrik de Keyser made remarkable sculptures of insane men and women for the cathedral of 's Hertogenbosch; his masterpiece, however, was the tomb of the Prince of Orange at Delft (p. 268), with its two figures of the prince, one as he appeared in life, and the other in death. After his death de Keyser's sons tried to maintain the fame of his workshop, but failed. Giovanni da Bologna (otherwise known as Jean de Boulogne), a native of Douai, left his home to work in Italy, as did Adriaen de Vries of Holland, who became court sculptor to Emperor Rudolph in Prague. It was the Flemings, and especially the talented Rombout Verhulst, who returned from their travels to introduce three-dimensional Baroque to the Northern Netherlands. Verhulst specialized in ornamental tombs, in which a sense of reality revealed itself in a heavy but imposing style (p. 274).

The Catholic Church and the aristocracy of the South maintained a higher rate of public commissions than the Protestant North. But even before the Reformation the North was already more inclined to be modest, more marked by the taste of merchants and farmers than by that of priests and courtiers. The contrast between North and South did not mean that art flourished less in the North. Less dominated by the Renaissance or by great personalities such as Rubens, the private collector stimulated artistic activity. There were some great talents, and many good, craftsmanlike minor artists. The remarkable group-portrait was a typical feature of Northern art, becoming fashionable through the tastes of the prosperous middle-class.

The painting of the 17th century

In the painting of the 17th century is an intimate, realistic sense of commonplace life, in which neither the aesthetic principles of the Renaissance nor the bravura of the Baroque played a part. The motives were determined by directness of vision and a life confined within narrow limits. Frans Hals modified the conventions of the group-portrait (p. 161) in a way which was later immediately recognized and appreciated by the Impressionists of the 19th century. His observation of men was acute and pitiless, but was saved from harshness by the breadth of his vision.

Rembrandt

In the 17th century Rembrandt van Ryn, by the increasing profundity of his artistic personality and the magic of his painting, excelled all that his country had so far produced. Nothing can compare with the series of self-portraits in which he succeeded in expressing all his joy in life, his sensuality, his griefs, and finally the utter rejection of vanity in his total loneliness. His drawing was magnificent; his sense of life is depicted in *The Polish Horseman, The Jewish Bride*, and the *Portrait of Hendrickje Stoffels* among countless others, intimate and thrilling. His *chiaroscuro* is essentially an expression of a metaphysical concept of light and shade. *The Night Watch* had already proved how his personal, highly Baroque interpretation of light and shade dominated his portraiture. Disappointed with the result, the sitters proved unable to comprehend his artistic flight. His experience of light was not of a static phenomenon, unlike that of van Eyck who displayed clarity even in shadows. Instead, he saw it grow from an indefinite darkness and rise to an increasing brilliance. In Rembrandt the light is a varying scale of twilights in which man participates spiritually as well as physically.

Jan Vermeer of Delft was also concerned with achieving a sensation of light in painting. For him and for Rembrandt's pupil Carel Fabritius, also an artist of Delft, the problems of painting light were a constant preoccupation. Vermeer became the poet of Dutch life. His art was a matter of choice, of seizing on the characteristic and intimate moments of everyday life in Delft. Vermeer would paint a woman in some ordinary room at an unimportant moment — pouring milk (p. 177), reading a note, making lace, quietly busy with a small task — for only then did he see the essential. His interiors and figures, not standing in light, but undergoing and absorbing it as they would the wind and rain, display a harmony which is his special characteristic.

The atmosphere of the 18th century

The 18th century brought a note of complacent satiety in sculpture as well as in painting. A weakened creative instinct was attended by an urge to collect, an increasing interest in museums, and the development of historical investigation. The elegance of life, and the rather scandalous doings of certain citizens, gave such artists as Cornelis Troost (p. 190) themes for a refined but rather petty art, seen even in their portrait painting. Landscape and townscape were topographically accurate and technically competent, but the century was one of minor artists.

19th century painters

In the 19th century, Holland and Belgium, now two consolidated but independent states, took part in their own way in the general streams of romantic and classic art, though without equaling the English landscape school of Constable and Turner, or such French artists as David, Géricault, or Ingres. David, the great French portrait painter and recorder of the Revolutionary and Napoleonic eras, emigrated to Brussels in 1815 and greatly influenced the local painters. A strong national element came into being. Gustave Wappers, Gallait and van Bree satisfied the demand for historical pieces, a fashion started in Holland by Jan Willem Pieneman. Hendrik Leys introduced a medieval tone and a sense of style that the other painters lacked. Of portrait painters François Navez, interpreting the manner of David, and the lesser artist Ary Scheffer of Dordrecht, painting portraits and romantically inclined religious pictures in Paris, enjoyed considerable reputations in Europe for a time, but these soon faded.

The influence of French art

The French influence of the Barbizon School and of Gustave Courbet helped to rescue Dutch painting from provincialism. The art of landscape painting, following the Barbizon School, regained importance through the masters of Tervueren, among them Hippolyte Boulenger, and the Hague School, which included the Maris brothers and Jan Hendrik Weissenbruch. One of the three Maris brothers, Matthijs, became a dreamy romantic who, turning from the world in disgust, eventually found anonymity and obscurity in the crowded city of London. His great talents were dissipated in the production of vague dreamlike figures.

Inspired by such artists as Jean François Millet and Honoré Daumier in France, Charles de Groux, Joseph Israels, and the painter-sculptor Constantin Meunier, who produced the *Monument to Labor* (p. 279), made the working man, whether as peasant or artisan, an important motif in their work. The trend culminated in the work of Vincent van Gogh, whose versatility anticipated the Expressionism and Fauvism of the 20th century. He broke with socially acceptable standards of art and was the first Dutch painter to reveal a human passion in his work since Rembrandt had given Dutch painting its world-wide significance. In Johan Barthold Jongkind, too, Holland produced an important painter to whom Impressionism was greatly indebted. Starting from a small local landscape-romanticism he achieved a personal art directly inspired by nature. His work greatly influenced the young Frenchman Claude Monet, the leader of the Impressionist movement.

James Ensor

The outstanding figure in Belgium was James Ensor. Belgium, more than Holland, had artists who, in the borderlands of reality and imagination found motifs that might be called latently surrealist. This can be seen in the almost frightening moods of Henri de Braekeleer and the subtle melancholy of Guillaume Vogels. But Ensor surpassed them all in his visionary rendering of human vice, of the joys and terrors of life. A painter of moralities, a second Bosch, he unmasked life by his play with carnival masks, endowing them with unpredictable functions, and displaying through them his dread of mass emotion, his hatred of man's hypocrisy.

Under the influence of Les XX, Brussels in the Post-Impressionist era experienced for a while a reflection of the Parisian and European avant-garde. Ensor was the Belgian symbol of this transition, but French "Division-ism" had its northern adherents too, among them the talented young Jan Toorop (p. 252), whose artistic personality united the Neo-Impressionistic and Symbolist trends, and Johan Thorn Prikker, who by his semi-orn-amental, semi-Expressionist stylizations became an in-fluence in Germany.

Tradition, though freed from academic conventions, remained an indestructible element in Dutch art. The last quarter of the 19th century saw the birth of an imposing and skillful Post-Impressionism that touched the old motives of still-life, town view, and human figure with a new spirit. Among the artists of this period were notably George Hendrik Breitner, Floris Verster, Suze Robertson, and Isaac Israels—painters whose profound color schemes and passionate pictorial styles place them unmistakably within the tradition of the Netherlands.

Biographies

SOME BOOKS FOR FURTHER READING

K. van Mander, *Het Schilderboek*, Haarlem, 1604.
(English translation in: C. van der Wall, *Dutch and Flemish Painters*, New York, 1936.)

J. Lassaigne and R. L. Delevoy, *Catalogue of Early Flemish, Dutch, and Flemish Paintings*, Metropolitan Museum of Art, New York, 1947.

E. Panofsky, *Early Netherlandish Painting*, 2 vols., Cambridge, Mass., 1953.

M. J. Friedländer, *From Van Eyck to Bruegel*, London, 1956.

Flemish Painting, 2 vols., Éditions d'Art Albert Skira, Geneva, 1958.

SEE ALSO UNDER THE INDIVIDUAL BIOGRAPHIES

PIETER AERTSEN 1508-1575

An important Romanist of the Dutch school

Pieter Aertsen is sometimes known by his nickname "Lange Pier," a reference to the height of the figures in his pictures. He was born in Amsterdam in 1508, the son of a stocking weaver, and for this reason used to sign his work with a wool comb. As a child he showed artistic ability, and was apprenticed to Alaert Claessen, with whom he remained until he had acquired a basic understanding of painting. He then traveled throughout the Netherlands, moving from place to place for 18 years.

Aertsen eventually settled in Antwerp and was admitted to the Guild of St. Luke in 1535. Seven years later he bought citizenship rights and married. In 1553 Aertsen returned to Amsterdam, where he applied for an important commission for the Oude Kerk. In 1566 the Calvinists and their sympathizers rioted, sacking churches and destroying religious paintings. Most of Aertsen's work for churches was destroyed at this time.

Although he returned to Antwerp for a while, he spent his last years in Amsterdam, dying there in 1575. Among his pupils were his three sons and his wife's nephew, Joachim Bueckelaer. Like all artists of his time, Aertsen painted religious works, but early in his career vegetables, fruit, and meat formed an important realistic element in his compositions at the expense of religious motifs. Aertsen developed the colorful style of the Antwerp Romanists into a more realistic representation of Dutch life.

L. van Puyvelde   The Flemish Primitives   Brussels, 1948

The Adoration of the Shepherds
(detail)
Amsterdam, Rijksmus.

HIS WORKS INCLUDE

Christ in the House of Martha
and Mary, 1553
Rotterdam, Boymans-van Beuningen
The Pannekoeckebackerye, 1560
Rotterdam, Boymans-van Beuningen
Woman at the Vegetable Stall, 1567
West Berlin, Staatl. Mus.

See also page 151

BALTHASAR VAN DER AST before 1590 - after 1656

A painter of highly detailed still-lifes

Balthasar van der Ast was born in Middelburg some time before 1590. He became the brother-in-law and probably the pupil of Ambrosius Bosschaert. He worked in Utrecht, and after 1632 in Delft. His paintings are minutely elaborate. They mostly show flowers, often with fruit, exotic shells, and lizards. His compositions are very modest, with a unifying silver-gray tone. Van der Ast's paintings are related stylistically to the paintings of Jan Bruegel, who, because of the smooth, fine texture of his work, was called "Velvet" Bruegel.

I. Bergström   Dutch Still-life Painting in the 17th Century   London, 1956
L.J. Bol   The Bosschaert Dynasty: Painters of Flowers   Leigh-on-Sea, England, 1960

HIS WORKS INCLUDE

Still-life, 1622
Cambridge, England, Fitzwm.
Still-life, 1623
Copenhagen, Statens Mus.
Still-life, 1655
London, coll. Dr. E. Sklarz

See also page 162

Winter Scene with Skaters near a
Castle, about 1609
London, N. G.

HENDRICK AVERCAMP 1585-1634

A painter of the winter scene

Hendrick Avercamp was born in 1585. He became a pupil of Pieter Isaaksz in
Amsterdam, and after 1625 he was active in Kampen. At first Avercamp was influenced by the Flemish landscapes of Pieter Bruegel the Elder and Gillis van
Coninxloo. This is noticeable in his use of the high-placed horizon, strong perspective, and his liking for circular compositions. Later he became independent of
the Flemings and made the transition to the realistic Dutch landscape characteristic of the 17th century.

Avercamp specialized in winter landscapes and skating scenes, in which he
achieved atmosphere by his use of subdued color with brilliant accents in the
figures. In his compositions there are often anecdotal elements. In addition to his
oil paintings, Avercamp produced some delicate watercolors. His nephew Barent
Avercamp was his pupil and close imitator.

N. Maclaren   The Dutch School, N. G. Catalogue   London, 1960

HIS WORKS INCLUDE

Winter Landscape
Amsterdam, Rijksmus.

Pleasures on the Ice
London, Leonard Koetser Gall.

Winter Landscape
St. Louis, City Art Mus.

See also page 150

Scene on Ice, about 1615
London, N. G.

Still-life with Lobster
Oxford, Ashmolean

ABRAHAM HENDRICKZ VAN BEYEREN about 1621-1690

A painter famous for his still-lifes of fish

Abraham Hendrickz van Beyeren was born at The Hague about 1621. He was one
of the most vivacious still-life painters of the second half of the 17th century in
Holland. In his early more sober kitchen paintings and fish still-lifes his use of
monochrome was similar to that of Pieter Claesz. Van Beyeren worked in Delft
from 1657 to 1661, and later at The Hague, and in Alkmaar, Amsterdam, Gouda,
and Overschie. In 1656 he took part in the foundation of the Confrérie Pictura at
The Hague.

His well-arranged still-lifes of breakfasts, flowers, and fish, and the kitchen
scenes of his mature style, are executed in bright and warm colors, mostly with soft
brownish-gray backgrounds. Although he at first followed Flemish traditions in
flower and fruit still-lifes, he later developed a rich style of color and composition.

Under the influence of Jan Davidsz de Heem, his works from about 1650 became more crowded and detailed. His extremely realistic fish paintings had a great influence on the succeeding generation.

I. Bergström   Dutch Still-life Painting in the 17th Century   London, 1956

HIS WORKS INCLUDE

Still-life
Amsterdam, Rijksmus.
Still-life
Dundee, Scotland, City Art Gall.

See also page 183

GIOVANNI DA BOLOGNA   1529-1608

A Florentine Mannerist sculptor

Samson, about 1567
London, V. and A.

Although he was born at Douai and started his career at Antwerp, Jean Boulogne, better known by the Italian name Giovanni da Bologna or Giambologna, arrived in Rome in 1545 and spent the rest of his life in Italy. He lived in Florence from 1553 until his death in 1608. Since Northern Europe was at this time much influenced by the Italian style imported into France by Francis I, Giambologna was already an Italian at second hand when he arrived in Rome, and was at once further influenced by Michelangelo. He became a great Mannerist sculptor, developing a style that is unmistakable. Voluptuous curves, elongated limbs, and very small heads make for simple shapes with clearly defined contours, delicate and sinuous. He is best known for his small scale works, although he carved a number of large statues, many of which were intended for the formal gardens of the Florentine villas of the period. Among his most famous works are the *Neptune Fountain* in Bologna, and the *Rape of the Sabine Women* in the Loggia dei Lanzi in Florence.

J. Pope-Hennessy   Italian High Renaissance and Baroque Sculpture   London, 1963

A River God (terracotta study)
London, V. and A.

HIS WORKS INCLUDE

Mercury, 1564
Florence, Mus. Naz. del Bargello
Fountain of Neptune, about 1567
Bologna
Venus
Florence, Villa della Petraja
Venus Bathing
Florence, Mus. Naz. del Bargello
River God
Florence, Mus. Naz. del Bargello

See also page 266

JAN BORMAN the ELDER   about 1450 - about 1522

A prolific woodcarver with an elaborate style

Jan Borman the Elder was an eminent woodcarver who worked in Brussels from about 1479 to 1520. He carved many rich and elaborate works for churches in Brussels and Louvain, and also in Germany and Sweden. Borman taught many other sculptors, and in 1479 he was given the citizenship of Brussels, although it was not his native town.

HIS WORKS INCLUDE

St. John the Evangelist, 1491
Louvain, St. Jacques
Mary Altar, 1513-21
Lübeck, Marienkirche

See also page 261

Altarpiece of St. George (detail) 1493
Brussels, Mus. Royaux d'Art et d'Histoire

In 1491 Borman completed the statue of *St. John the Evangelist* for the altar of the Church of St. Jacques in Louvain. Two years later he produced his masterpiece, the *Altarpiece of St. George*, for Notre Dame Cathedral in Louvain. This magnificent work, which represents the martyrdom of St. George, is both carved and painted. In 1494 he carved a crucifix for the rood-screen of St. Sulpice in Paris.

Between 1507 and 1510 Borman worked in partnership with the shrinemaker, Peterceels, on two altarpieces for which they had been commissioned. During the same period Borman was given the commission for altar carvings for the oratorium of the brewers' guild in the Church of St. Pierre in Louvain. He was helped in this work by his brother Willem, who was a well-known carver in his own right.

Borman produced some decorations for houses in Brussels and Louvain about 1510. Between 1513 and 1521 he executed varied pieces of work, including the *Mary Altar* for the Marienkirche in Lübeck. In 1522 he completed his magnificent *Passion Altar* for the Parish Church of Güstrow at Mecklenburg in Germany, on which the painted decorations were probably by Bernaert van Orley.

Church Interior
Haarlem, Teyler's Mus.

Vestry at Nimeguen (detail)
Amsterdam, Rijksmus.

JOHANNES BOSBOOM   1817-1891

A painter who specialized in painting church interiors

Johannes Bosboom was born at The Hague on February 18, 1817. In 1831 he was a pupil in the studio of Bartholomeus Johannes van Hove, a painter who specialized in town views and theatrical decorations. In these early years Bosboom also worked on theatrical decor, an interest that was to influence his later painting.

In 1831 Bosboom traveled through the Rhineland, where he stayed for some time in Cologne and Coblenz. Soon afterwards he visited France, where he made numerous drawings and studies, particularly in Paris and Rouen. These sketches were later worked up into paintings. In 1850 he journeyed through north Brabant, visiting different churches and monasteries, and sketching them as he traveled.

A year later Bosboom married a celebrated authoress of historical novels, A. L. Toussaint, and they settled at The Hague. He pursued a successful career, and received several international awards. He died on September 14, 1891. Bosboom's best-known paintings are of church interiors which frequently have figures in 17th-century costume, but he also painted landscapes, town views, and peasant scenes. The influence of Rembrandt's work may be seen in his paintings.

HIS WORKS INCLUDE

Interior of the Bakenesserkerk at Haarlem, 1875
London, N. G.

Interior of the Cathedral at Trier
Amsterdam, Rijksmus.

Church Interior
Amsterdam, Rijksmus.

See also page 238

HIERONYMUS BOSCH   about 1450-1516

A richly imaginative painter of allegorical scenes

Hieronymus van Aeken Bosch is well known as a painter of fantastic and macabre allegories, rich in inventive detail. He was one of a family of painters, originally from Aachen (Aix-la-Chapelle), hence van Aeken; his last name derives from the town of 's Hertogenbosch (Bois-le-Duc) where he lived and died. Born about 1450, Bosch was trained possibly by his father, or by his grandfather Jan van Aeken who painted a fresco of *The Crucifixion* in 's Hertogenbosch cathedral. Bosch himself painted some altarpieces for the cathedral and made some designs for stained glass and tapestries. None of these survive, however.

The style of his early paintings, for example *The Crucifixion* and *The Conjuror*, was surprisingly remote from the strong trends of contemporary Flemish art, harking back instead to the traditional manner established by the Master of Flémalle and Roger van der Weyden 50 years before. Bosch's work, however, was forward looking as well as retrospective. His rendering of light and feeling for spatial composition, the illusion he achieves of depth and distance, are reminiscent of the work of Jan and Hubert van Eyck, but they also anticipate the work of the late 16th-century painters, both in the Netherlands and in Italy. In the next generation the fantastic, rocky landscapes of the Flemish painter, Joachim Patenier, owed much to Bosch.

Bosch's great theme, fully developed in *The Garden of Delights*, was temptation and all its apparatus, expressed in apocalyptic, dreamlike compositions full of

ANONYMOUS
Portrait of Hieronymus Bosch
Arras, Bibl. Municipale

The Temptation of St. Anthony (detail)
Madrid, Prado

HIS WORKS INCLUDE

The Adoration of the Magi,
about 1495
Madrid, Prado

The Last Judgment, about 1504
Munich, Alte Pin.

Christ Carrying the Cross, about 1505
Ghent, Mus. des B-A.

St. Jerome in Prayer, about 1505
Ghent, Mus. des B-A.

The Nativity
Cologne, Wallraf-Richartz-Mus.

St. John on Patmos
West Berlin, Staatl. Mus.

The Adoration of the Magi
New York, Met. Mus.

See also pages 141, 213, 214, 215

21

lurking devils and pregnant with medieval symbolism. His paintings have no apparent precedent, although the gestures of the many small figures that people his canvases recall medieval art, particularly Romanesque sculpture. Some of Bosch's *Danse Macabre* subjects had dominated popular woodcut design since the Black Death of the previous century, and were to be taken up by Albrecht Dürer in an engraving entitled *The Knight, Death, and the Devil* and by Hans Holbein the Younger in 1538 in his woodcut series, *The Dance of Death*. The first artist to draw

Christ on the Cross, early work
Brussels, Mus. Royaux des B-A.

The Prodigal Son
Rotterdam, Boymans-van Beuningen

The Crowning with Thorns, early work
London, N. G.

The Temptation of St. Anthony:
left panel of triptych, about 1500
Lisbon, Mus. Nacional de Arte Antiga

The Temptation of St. Anthony:
right panel of triptych, about 1500
Lisbon, Mus. Nacional de Arte Antiga

creative inspiration from Bosch was Pieter Bruegel the Elder, two generations later.

Many of Bosch's paintings are in the form of altarpieces, and it is therefore possible that they were commissioned by the Brotherhood of Our Lady in 's Hertogenbosch, to which he belonged for 30 years. It has been suggested that he may have been a member of a secret and orgiastic sect called the Adamists, and that these extraordinary paintings are illustrations of their heretical dogmas.

W. Fraenger   The Millenium of Hieronymus Bosch   Chicago, 1951
C. Linfert   Hieronymus Bosch: The Paintings   New York, 1959

The Hay-Cart (detail)
Madrid, Prado

DIERIC BOUTS   about 1415-1475

A painter of Louvain

Dieric Bouts was born about 1415 in Haarlem. He probably received his early training under Albert van Ouwater. He married his first wife in Louvain and lived there until his death in 1475. Late in life he was to marry again. In Louvain he came under the influence of Roger van der Weyden, city painter of Brussels, with whom he probably worked. Bouts's paintings of about 1440 to 1450 resemble those of Petrus Christus, whom he met either in Haarlem or Bruges.

Bouts's figures possess a stiff, somewhat Gothic formality, but at the same time, as for instance in his *Martyrdom of St. Erasmus*, his pictures are charged with great emotion, making the sad, still faces seem quite inadequate. Bouts tended to use deliberately restrained colors, and he exploited the possibilities of perspective in order to combine the separate elements of the picture into a coherent whole. In

Portrait of a Man, 1462
London, N. G.

HIS WORKS INCLUDE
The Nativity, about 1445
Madrid, Prado
The Resurrection, before 1464
Munich, Alte Pin.
The Martyrdom of St. Erasmus,
before 1466
Louvain, St. Pierre
The Last Supper, about 1467
Louvain, St. Pierre
The Deposition, 1470
Paris, Louvre
The Justice of Emperor
Otto, 1470-75
Brussels, Mus. Royaux des B-A.

See also pages 134, 212

The Entombment (detail) about 1455
London, N. G.

The Madonna and Child with
St. Peter and St. Paul, about 1462
London, N. G.

this respect his work is reminiscent of Jan van Eyck. One of his masterpieces, *The Last Supper*, which he painted in about 1467, illustrates these compositional qualities.

In 1468 Bouts was appointed city painter of Louvain. The town council at once commissioned from him two large compositions for their council chamber. The subjects of these compositions are *The Last Judgment* and two scenes from the legend of *The Justice of Emperor Otto*. In 1472 he undertook another large work, *The Martyrdom of St. Hippolytus*, but he died before the work was finished. The Ghent painter, Hugo van der Goes, was called in four years later to value the picture, and he completed it.

Dieric Bouts had two sons, Dieric and Albrecht, who worked with their father in Louvain as painters and illuminators. Albrecht's *Assumption* is the only work which can be ascribed with any certainty to either brother. The picture was identified by his coat of arms, and a record of the painting appears in a contemporary document.

H.B. Wehle and M. Salinger   *Early Flemish, Dutch, and German Paintings*
    Met. Mus. Catalogue   Cambridge, Mass., 1947
M. Davies   *The Early Netherlandish School, N. G. Catalogue*   London, 1955

The Painter-Restorer, 1878
Antwerp, Mus. Royal des B-A.

Henri De Braekeleer

HIS WORKS INCLUDE

Dining Room in Leys' House, 1869
Antwerp, Mus. Royal des B-A.
Man in a Chair, 1875
Antwerp, Mus. Royal des B-A.
Man at the Window, 1876
Brussels, Mus. Royaux des B-A.
Strawberries and Champagne, 1883
Antwerp, Mus. Royal des B-A.

See also pages 195, 239

HENRI DE BRAEKELEER   1840-1888

A painter of intimate genre scenes of Antwerp

Henri de Braekeleer was born in Antwerp on June 11, 1840, the son of Ferdinand de Braekeleer the Elder, who was a history and genre painter of Antwerp, a member of the Belgian Academy, and keeper of the Antwerp Museum. Braekeleer started painting at an early age under the influence of his uncle, Hendrik Leys. He took lessons at the Antwerp Academy, and studied with his father and his uncle. He devoted himself to scenes of everyday life in Antwerp, and scarcely left his studio, except for walks in the city.

In 1861 Braekeleer exhibited his first pictures, *The Laundry* and *The Coppersmith's Workshop*, in Antwerp. These works show how strongly he was influenced by Dutch old masters, particularly Pieter de Hooch. He visited Germany in 1862, and spent some weeks in Holland, probably about 1869 or 1870. For the greater part of his career he remained under the influence of the Flemish and German primitives, and the 17th-century Dutch "Intimistes." He won a gold medal in Brussels in 1872 for *The Geographer* and *The Lesson*, and another gold medal in Vienna the following year for *The Painter's Studio*.

For the most part Braekeleer's paintings were unpretentious, and executed with great attention to detail. His color was perhaps too muddy in tone. He used an extremely restricted palette, the paintings invariably being executed in siennas, browns, ochers, blacks, and whites. His perception of light, however, was very subtle. Suddenly, in the last years of his life, he began to paint with a frenzy of color, as a result of seeing works by Édouard Manet and the Impressionists. His

The Geographer, about 1872
Brussels, Mus. Royaux des B-A.

View of Antwerp (detail)
Antwerp, Mus. Royal des B-A.

palette became much freer, composed of pure colors. Unfortunately his reason gave way, and in 1888 his family was forced to have him interned in an asylum, where he died on June 20, 1888, at the age of 48.

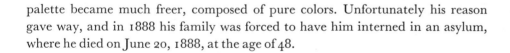

GEORGE HENDRIK BREITNER   1857-1923

A painter of military scenes and Amsterdam life

George Hendrik Breitner was born in Rotterdam in 1857. He went in 1876 to the Academy of The Hague. In 1880 he worked in the studio of Willem Maris and in 1881 with Hendrik Willem Mesdag. Three years later he was in Paris for a short while at Cormon's Atelier, and finally he went to the Amsterdam Academy.

Though Breitner is classified as a Dutch Impressionist, his paintings are nearly expressionist in their restless, passionate, and fierce execution. He was in contact with Vincent van Gogh while he was at The Hague but was not influenced by him. Breitner's themes are unusual for his time. For the most part he painted the views and urban life of Amsterdam in a realistic manner, quite unlike the quiet, lyrical landscapes of Jakob Maris or Anton Mauve, or the Hague School in general.

Breitner also painted military scenes, portraits, a series of girls in Japanese kimonos, and some nudes and still-lifes. His palette was mostly dark and earthbound,

Light Artillery
Amsterdam, Rijksmus.

with contrast provided by splashes of vivid color. After 1905 his activity declined and his work lost its impetuosity and fire. During his great years he was among the most successful artists of the time. He is said to have been passionately dissatisfied with the dominance of *la petite bourgeoisie*, and he was also an admirer of Émile Zola. He died in 1923.

The Workmen's Meal
Amsterdam, Rijksmus.

The Wooden Shoes
Amsterdam, Rijksmus.

MELCHIOR BROEDERLAM   active 1381 - about 1409

An early Flemish artist

Melchior Broederlam was the earliest painter to work in a recognizably Flemish style. Born probably in Ypres, he became court painter to Philip the Bold, Duke of Burgundy, in 1385. His tasks, which were typical of the work of a medieval artist, included the painting of a carved altarpiece, designing tiled floors, painting banners, and decorating a pavilion with gold leaf.

Between 1390 and 1393 Broederlam was in Paris, where he was commissioned to paint two wings of an altarpiece. These were completed in 1399. In contrast to the two-dimensional "wallpaper" effects achieved by earlier artists of France and Flanders, they show the influence of the new International Gothic style, which owed much to Simone Martini. Broederlam's influence is reflected in a small but important group of Flemish illuminated books. He died in 1409 or possibly later.

G. Ring   A Century of French Painting   London, 1949

ADRIAEN BROUWER

A founder of the "low-life" school in the Netherlands

Adriaen Brouwer was born in Oudenaarde in Flanders in 1605 or 1606. His parents were poor, probably as a result of the prolonged religious wars with Spain. It may have been from his father, a designer of tapestries from whom he had his first instruction, that he inherited his interest in drawing.

In 1622 Brouwer went to Antwerp, where he trained as a painter, probably in the circle of Pieter Bruegel the Younger. His earliest works may have been based on Pieter Bruegel the Elder's village scenes. He went to Haarlem in 1625, and then on to Amsterdam. In Haarlem he met Frans Hals and worked in his studio at the same time as Adriaen van Ostade. Ostade and Brouwer together founded the "low-life" school of Dutch painting. They had a great influence on the Dutch and Flemish genre painters, and especially on Jan Steen and David Teniers the Younger. Typical of Brouwer's work are tavern scenes of boorish merrymaking. Their delicacy of color and breadth of handling compensate for the grossness of their subjects. Brouwer also painted a number of landscapes.

About 1632 Brouwer returned to Antwerp, where he joined the painters' guild and came under the influence, especially in his use of color, of Peter Paul Rubens. In 1633 he was imprisoned by the Spanish for spying; the prison baker, Joos van Craesbeeck, became his pupil and imitator. Brouwer died, at the age of 33, outside an Antwerp tavern.

HIS WORKS INCLUDE

Drinkers Sitting in a Courtyard, about 1631
Brussels, Mus. Royaux des B-A.

Smokers and Drinkers in a Tavern, about 1631
Munich, Alte Pin.

Moonlight on the Dunes, about 1636
West Berlin, Staatl. Mus.

Peasants Brawling
Dresden, Gemäldegal.

The Sense of Hearing
Munich, Alte Pin.

See also page 174

A Boor Asleep
London, Wallace Coll.

Three Boors Drinking
London, N. G.

Portrait of a Man
The Hague, Mauritshuis

27

PIETER BRUEGEL the YOUNGER 1564-1637/38
JAN BRUEGEL the ELDER 1568-1625

The artist sons of Pieter Bruegel the Elder

Pieter Bruegel the Younger was born in Brussels in 1564. As a young man he studied with Gillis van Coninxloo in Antwerp, where in 1585 he was registered as a master in the painters' guild. Jan, Pieter's brother, was born in 1568, also in Brussels. Their father, Pieter Bruegel the Elder, died when his older son was only five. It is therefore unlikely that Pieter Bruegel the Younger saw the originals of his father's best paintings. It is probable that his work, which closely resembled his father's, was derived either from prints or from the work of his father's imitators.

The younger Pieter Bruegel specialized in genre scenes and fantastic paintings of hell that followed the satirical tradition of his father. He became known as "Hell" Bruegel. His work did not consist exclusively of copies of his father's paintings, but he produced infinite variations on them. There is no perceptible development in his art, although the earlier paintings are more delicate in execution. Unlike Jan Bruegel, Pieter the Younger does not seem to have traveled.

Jan and Pieter sometimes worked together, but Jan enjoyed the greater reputation during his lifetime. He painted landscapes, fruit, and flowers of so fine a texture that he was nicknamed "Velvet" Bruegel. He traveled to Italy and worked in Rome. In 1597 he was employed by Cardinal Bartolommeo in Milan. He resided for a time in Cologne on his return journey, but by 1600 he was established in

**PIETER BRUEGEL
the YOUNGER** The Adoration of
the Kings (detail)
Amsterdam, Rijksmus.

PIETER BRUEGEL the YOUNGER
The Village Fête, 1632
Cambridge, England, Fitzwm.

28

Antwerp, where he married Isabella de Jose. His eldest son, Jan the Younger, also a painter, was born in 1601. "Velvet" Bruegel occupied important positions in the painters' guild of Antwerp, and was also a friend of Rubens, with whom he collaborated.

H. Gerson and E. H. ter Kuile   Art and Architecture in Belgium 1600-1800   London, 1960

HIS WORKS INCLUDE
JAN BRUEGEL the ELDER
The Flight into Egypt, 1607
Leningrad, Hermitage
Village Scene, 1608
Turin, Gall. Sabauda
Still-life, 1618
Brussels, Mus. Royaux des B-A.

See also page 222

JAN BRUEGEL the ELDER
Terrestrial Paradise, about 1613
Paris, Louvre

JAN BRUEGEL the ELDER
The Rest on the Flight into Egypt
(detail) about 1595
The Hague, Mauritshuis

PIETER BRUEGEL the ELDER   about 1525-1569

A painter of genre scenes and religious subjects set in vast landscapes

Pieter Bruegel the Elder was born about 1525 in a village near Breda. He became a master in the Antwerp painters' guild in 1551, and shortly afterwards went to France and Italy. In 1553 he was in Rome and the next year he returned to the Netherlands, crossing the Alps on his journey. The mountains and the scenery of Italy made an immense impression on him, noticeable in the drawings he made at the time. They were extremely influential in the development of his landscape style. Bruegel's earliest known painting is *Naples Harbor*, now in the Galleria Doria, Rome. Bruegel also studied painting under Pieter Coeck, whose daughter he married. After spending some time in Antwerp, he moved to Brussels, where he remained for the rest of his life.

Pieter Bruegel the Elder was the first of a family of notable painters. His two

The Painter and The Connoisseur
(detail) about 1565
Vienna, Albertina

The Adoration of the Kings, 1564
London, N. G.

BRVEGEL

sons, Pieter the Younger ("Hell" Bruegel) and Jan ("Velvet" Bruegel), became well known in their own right. Other members of the family are remembered as still-life painters. Little is known about the life of Bruegel the Elder, but there is no doubt whatever about the originality of his vision and the brilliance of his technique. Most of the Flemish painters of his time were strongly influenced by the fashions of contemporary Italian art, but Bruegel created an entirely individual manner. His iconography was also new. *The Adoration of the Kings*, 1564, shows how sharply Bruegel departed from the traditional restraint that would have been considered fitting by earlier artists dealing with the same or a similar Biblical theme.

Bruegel's early work shows the influence of Hieronymus Bosch's fantastic, symbolic paintings. Bruegel was clearly intrigued by the fantasies woven by Bosch, and he began a series of engravings in the manner of Bosch, using such subjects as *The Seven Virtues and the Seven Vices*. He also began a series of large paintings which display both the influence of Bosch's work and his own interest in the habits and customs of the peasants. He viewed his subjects with a satirical eye. The earlier paintings show crowds of minute figures busily occupied, but in his later work a more massive style develops, with fewer figures depicted on a larger scale. This may be seen in four landscapes, three in Vienna and one in New York, which were probably designed to illustrate the seasons. In these the manner is more natural and they give a clear idea of village life of his day.

Bruegel's last works, such as *The Parable of the Blind Leading the Blind*, *The Peasant Dance*, and *The Peasant Wedding*, are superb representations of this same peasant life,

Summer (detail) 1568
Hamburg, Kunsthalle

The Beekeepers and the Nest Thief,
about 1565
West Berlin, Staatl. Mus.

The Carrying of the Cross, 1564
Vienna, Kunsthist. Mus.

The Tower of Babel (detail)
about 1563
Vienna, Kunsthist. Mus.

The Triumph of Death, about 1560
Madrid, Prado

The Gathering of the Herds (detail)
about 1565
Vienna, Kunsthist. Mus.

See also pages 146, 147, 148, 149, 217, 218

without the note of irony noticeable before, but certainly with a tale to tell. It is said that Bruegel destroyed a number of his pictures in case they incriminated his family. This is illustrative of the period in which he lived, for he was working while the Duke of Alva was ravaging the Netherlands. In many of Bruegel's surviving paintings there are indications of the brutalities to which the population was subjected. They show tortures, skeletons, gibbets, representations of Death claiming his victims, and every kind of horror, devastation, and misery. It is perhaps surprising that Bruegel himself escaped the punishment that his work might so easily have brought him. He died in 1569.

O. Benesch   *The Art of the Renaissance in Northern Europe*   Cambridge, Mass., 1945
L. van Puyvelde   *Pieter Bruegel: The Dulle Griet*   London, 1945
A. J. Barnouw   *The Fantasy of Pieter Bruegel*   New York, 1947
G. Glück   *Pieter Bruegel the Elder*   London, 1951
Ch. de Tolnay   *The Drawings of Pieter Bruegel the Elder*   London, 1952
F. Grossman   *The Paintings of Bruegel*   London, 1955

PETRUS CHRISTUS

died 1472/73

A painter who continued the tradition of the van Eycks

Petrus Christus was a 15th-century painter in Bruges in the style of the brothers van Eyck. He came from his native Baerle to settle in Bruges, where he was probably taught by Jan van Eyck. In 1444, three years after Jan's death, he was admitted to the Guild of St. Luke in Bruges. There is a record that he made some copies of pictures in Cambrai Cathedral in France. He may have stopped there on his way to Italy, as a painter in Milan in 1457 known as "Piero di Burges," the Italian for Peter of Bruges, may well have been he. The painter Antonello da Messina shows strong Flemish tendencies in the virtuosity of his design. Yet he did

Portrait of a Young Man, about 1450-60
London, N. G.

The Lamentation
Brussels, Mus. Royaux des B-A.

not visit the Netherlands, and it is therefore reasonable to suggest that he was acquainted with "Piero di Burges" in Italy. The next record of Christus' activities is dated 1463, when he collaborated with an unknown artist on a painting to be used in a procession of the Confraternity of the Holy Blood in Bruges.

The composition of many of Christus' paintings is like that of the van Eycks, whose work he may consciously have copied. At that time imitation in painting was practiced to a greater degree than it is today, individuality now being all-important in art. Then it was thought perfectly honorable to continue a tradition established by an artist of the previous generation even if, as in Christus' case, this led to an archaic, heavy style.

In fact there is little likelihood of confusing his work with that of any other artist, because his figures, with their round heads and imperfectly drawn, plump hands, bear a definite family resemblance. Christus went further than the van Eycks in the exploration of perspective, and later, borrowing this time from Roger van der Weyden, in the portrayal of emotion. Petrus Christus sometimes signed his work with the inscription XPI, the Greek abbreviation for Christus.

M. Davies   The Early Netherlandish School, N. G. Catalogue   London, 1955

HIS WORKS INCLUDE

The Virgin and Child, about 1445
Budapest, Mus. of Fine Arts
Portrait of a Carthusian Monk, 1446
New York, Met. Mus.
Portrait of a Kneeling Donor, about 1446
Washington, D. C., N. G.
Portrait of a Lady of the Talbot Family, about 1446
West Berlin, Staatl. Mus.
The Madonna with Saints, 1457
Frankfurt-am-Main, Städelsches Kunstinst.

See also page 132

PIETER CLAESZ   1596-1661

A painter of mainly monochrome still-lifes

With Willem Claesz Heda, Pieter Claesz was the first painter of the monochrome still-lifes that were a feature of Dutch 17th-century painting. His themes were very

Still-life with Drinking Vessels, 1649
London, N. G.

Still-life with Golden Chain
Oxford, Ashmolean

simple, chiefly breakfast tables set with pewter plates, bread, oysters, and silver vessels, all against a plain background. Claesz achieved an atmosphere of utter stillness. At first he used some bright colors, but after 1630 only elaborate nuances of brown and gray with modest, soft colors.

Sometimes Claesz's paintings have a symbolic interpretation, usually of the vanity of earthly pleasures represented by the objects he depicted. Probably influenced by Frans Hals, Claesz developed a free touch, and his light effects became stronger and the compositions more open. After 1640 he again used a wider palette, but the whole impression remained one of monochrome. Claesz's earliest paintings date from 1623, his last from 1657.

I. Bergström Dutch Still-life Painting in the 17th Century London, 1956

JOOS VAN CLEVE
about 1485-1540/41

A painter of portraits and religious subjects

Joos van Cleve, also referred to as the Master of the Death of the Virgin, was born probably in 1485. His birthplace is unknown, but it is likely that he was a German from the ancient town of Cleves on the Lower Rhine. He seems to have been in Genoa during the rule of Philip of Cleves, from 1501 to 1506, and his interest in an Italianate style of painting stems from this period. He became a master in the Antwerp painters' guild in 1511.

Joos was a contemporary and rival of Quentin Massys, and many of the portraits attributed to him show a cool realism reminiscent of Massys or even Hans Holbein. Italian influence, principally that of Leonardo da Vinci, shows itself in his use of chiaroscuro, achieved by modeling his forms with opaque shading, in contrast to

Portrait of a Man
Amsterdam, Rijksmus.

The Death of the Virgin, 1515
Cologne, Wallraf-Richartz-Mus.

34

the delicate, transparent shading used by Hans Memling and the previous generation of painters.

Joos was elected dean of the Antwerp painters' guild in 1519 and again in 1525. He had a number of apprentices in his workshop between 1516 and his departure from the Netherlands in 1530. At this date he went to work at the French court, where he painted many portraits of Francis I and his queen. In 1536 he visited England, at the same time as Holbein, and painted the portrait of Henry VIII that is now at Hampton Court. In 1540 he was recalled to France to paint a group portrait of the royal family. His son, Cornelis van Cleve, was a painter of portraits and religious subjects.

E. G. Troche Painting in the Netherlands in the 15th and 16th Centuries London, 1936

Portrait of Henry VIII, 1536
London, Hampton Court, Royal Coll.

JOSEPH MENDES DA COSTA   1863-1939

A sculptor prominent in the Dutch artistic revival of the late 19th century

Joseph Mendes da Costa was born in 1863. As the son of a stonemason in Amsterdam, he learned the trade in his father's workshop. Later he studied at the Quellinus School for Sculptors and at the Amsterdam School of Applied Arts, where he met Lambertus Zijl. The two sculptors founded the Labor et Ars Society, the so-called L.E.A., which opposed the official academic teaching of the time.

After a period in which he pursued the applied arts, da Costa began to make small groups and figures in ceramic stoneware and terracotta. He found the subjects for these works, which are often anecdotal in character, in the daily life of the Jewish quarter of Amsterdam, and in the animal world. From 1907 to 1912 he made little sculptures of Old Testament figures such as Moses, Jeremiah, and Elias, and he also produced bronze statues of Spinoza, Vincent van Gogh, and Jan Steen.

The years about 1900 were a period of great architectural activity in the Netherlands, and da Costa produced decorative works and monumental sculptures, such as those for the buildings of the Utrecht Life Assurance Company in Amsterdam and Utrecht. These works reflect his ideal of the unity of sculpture and architecture.

Between 1915 and 1917 da Costa was commissioned to make monuments of General de Wet and President Steyn, and a group of bronze figures entitled *Love*. In his earlier small figures his style was impressionistic, but the later ceramic stoneware and bronze works and the monumental sculptures demonstrate his personal manner. They reveal a sense of pathos as well as a formalization of line in which there are elements of Art Nouveau. This style, once established, was typical of all his work. Da Costa died in 1939.

Tile with Figures (detail) 1900
Amsterdam, Stedelijk Mus.

HIS WORKS INCLUDE

The Salvation Trump of St. John, 1891
Otterlo, Holland, Kröller-Müller
Head of a Javanese, 1898
Otterlo, Holland, Kröller-Müller
King David, 1907
Otterlo, Holland, Kröller-Müller
Love, 1917
Otterlo, Holland, Kröller-Müller
Self-portrait, 1927
Otterlo, Holland, Kröller-Müller

See also page 277

Figures and Cows in a Meadow
(detail) about 1658
London, N. G.

HIS WORKS INCLUDE

A River Scene with Distant Windmills,
about 1645
London, N. G.

Portrait of a Bearded Man, 1649
London, N. G.

The Large Dort, about 1650
London, N. G.

Mountainous Landscape
Amsterdam, Rijksmus.

Cows by the Water
Budapest, Mus. of Fine Arts

See also page 235

AELBERT CUYP

An accomplished and versatile painter

Aelbert Cuyp was born in Dordrecht in 1620 and died there in 1691. He first studied under his father, an accomplished painter himself. Later Cuyp began to paint portraits of the citizens of Dordrecht, both men and women, often on horseback. These pictures date from about 1650. They are admirable studies of the life and costume of the period, both horses and their riders being painted with an obvious affection and with an attention to detail that never becomes tiresome.

Cuyp seems to have been a citizen of some standing. As a man of property around Dordrecht, he enjoyed the right to sit in the high court of the province, and in 1672 his name was among those chosen by William III, stadtholder of the Netherlands, to be a member of the regency of Dordrecht.

Cuyp's pictures are not often dated, and he seems to have ceased working about 1675. The pictures of his middle and later years are almost all signed with his full name, though there exist a number of doubtful authenticity, most of which are signed with his initials. The number of his works has been variously put between such wide limits as 300 and 800, but even the smaller of these two figures is probably too high.

Most of Cuyp's best compositions show animals, figures, and landscape bathed in a golden light. An example is the view of Dordrecht known as *The Large Dort*. His versatility is indicated by the grand sea-picture, *The Arrival of Maurice of Nassau at Scheveningen*. These two paintings give an idea of Cuyp's wonderful range. The one is all quietude and stillness, while the other, with its ships crowded with busy people, conveys the pomp of a great occasion.

W. Bode   The Great Masters of Flemish and Dutch Painting   London, 1909
N. Maclaren   The Dutch School, N. G. Catalogue   London, 1960

Ubbergen Castle, about 1655
London, N. G.

A Hilly River Landscape with a Horseman Talking
to a Shepherdess, about 1660
London, N. G.

GERARD DAVID

about 1450-1523

The last master of the Bruges school

Gerard David, a painter from Oudewater near Utrecht, was born about 1450. His style is so similar to that of Geertgen tot Sint Jans that it is supposed that they were fellow pupils of Albert van Ouwater in Haarlem. Like Hans Memling before him, he painted in Bruges most of his life. He was the last master of the Bruges school and was much in demand there. His work presents a paradox. He anticipated the Renaissance in emotional depth, while continuing the soft and solemn style of the previous century.

David settled in Bruges in 1483 and was admitted to the Guild of St. Luke in the following year. Three years after that he was engaged on paintings for the Town Hall. He also had a reputation as a fine miniaturist and worked in this capacity for the Duke of Burgundy. In 1496 he married Cornelia Cnoop, daughter of the dean of the Bruges goldsmiths' guild. Soon afterward he began work on two large paintings for the Court Hall, *The Judgment of Cambyses* and *The Punishment of Sisamnes*. These illustrated themes from the ancient Greek historian Herodotus, and were intended to urge the magistrates to be conscientious in their work.

During the latter half of the 15th century the waterways of Bruges gradually silted up, so that its shipping was restricted and its trade and prosperity passed to Antwerp. David, too, in 1515 moved from Bruges to Antwerp, and paid the necessary fee to have his name entered in the Antwerp register of painters. While living there he met Quentin Massys and Joachim Patenier. Later he returned to Bruges, where he died in 1523.

E. G. Troche   Painting in the Netherlands in the 15th and 16th Centuries   London, 1936
M. Davies   The Early Netherlandish School, N. G. Catalogue   London, 1955

The Deposition, after 1515
London, N. G.

HIS WORKS INCLUDE

The Judgment of Cambyses, 1498
Bruges, Mus. Communal

The Punishment of Sisamnes, 1498
Bruges, Mus. Communal

The Marriage at Cana, about 1503
Paris, Louvre

The Baptism of Christ, about 1507
Bruges, Mus. Communal

Sacra Conversazione, 1509
Rouen, Mus. des B-A.

The Annunciation, about 1520
Frankfurt-am-Main, Städelsches Kunstinst.

The Madonna and Child Enthroned with Two Angels
Basel, Kunstmus.

See also page 139

The Virgin and Child with Saints and Donor, about 1509
London, N. G.

The Adoration of the Kings (detail) after 1515
London, N. G.

Self-portrait (detail)
Amsterdam, Rijksmus.

GERARD DOU

A pupil of Rembrandt

Gerard Dou was born in Leiden in 1613, the son of a glazier, with whom he first worked. He was next apprenticed to an engraver and then went to Pieter Couwenhorn, a glass painter. Finally he became a pupil of the young Rembrandt, who was seven years his senior.

It is evident that Dou used the same models as his great master, and acquired from him more than a little of his superb technique. For some years Rembrandt's influence is obvious in the use of dramatic lighting and thickly applied paint. Later this influence weakened. Dou's pictures became crowded with minute and almost painfully exact detail, executed with the technique of a miniaturist and with a brilliant, enamel-like finish.

At this stage Dou began to paint interiors, often in candlelight. He is not, however, the equal of Gabriel Metsu, Gerard Terborch, or Jan Steen, with whom in many ways he can be compared, and this is largely due to his over-emphasis on detail. He also painted a number of Biblical subjects. Dou met with far greater success in his own lifetime than most of his contemporaries. He died in 1675 a very wealthy man, so it is clear that his paintings had appealed to rich clients.

N. Maclaren   The Dutch School, N. G. Catalogue   London, 1960

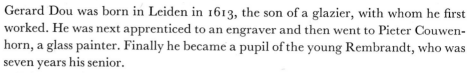

HIS WORKS INCLUDE

The Dentist, 1630
Paris, Louvre

Portrait of Johan Wittert van der Aa
1646
Amsterdam, Rijksmus.

The Doctor, about 1655
Luxembourg, Mus. Nat.

Portrait of a Young Woman,
about 1660
London, N. G.

See also page 234

The Young Mother, 1658
The Hague, Mauritshuis

Poulterer's Shop, about 1672
London, N. G.

FRANS DUQUESNOY

about 1594-1643

A sculptor important in the development of the Baroque style in the southern Netherlands

Frans Duquesnoy was born in Brussels about 1594, the son of the sculptor, Hieronymus Duquesnoy, whose pupil he became. In 1618 he was given a sum of money by the Archduke Ferdinand, in order to study sculpture in Rome. It was here that Duquesnoy developed his mature style, and produced his most important works.

In Rome, Duquesnoy came into contact with Gian Lorenzo Bernini and Nicolas Poussin, and he was also noticed by van Dyck, who painted his portrait. He was fortunate in finding good patrons. Filippo Colonna commissioned from him a large ivory crucifix for Pope Urban VIII, and the Marquis Vincentio Giustiniani bought from him several statues of mythological figures.

Pope Urban VIII employed Duquesnoy to produce bronze ornaments for St. Peter's, Rome, and also to carve a massive marble *St. Andrew* for one of the piers of the church. A small plaster model was ready in 1629, and the statue itself was finished by 1633. During the same period he made a marble *St. Susanna* for the Church of S. Maria di Loreto in Rome. Nothing else remains today of Duquesnoy's monumental works, but some small sculptures and reliefs depicting children in a style full of grace and charm still exist.

In spite of the patronage, Duquesnoy was not able to make a satisfactory living. After some deliberation he accepted an offer from Louis XIII to go to Paris, with guarantee of a fixed income, but he died in 1643 on the journey at Leghorn and was buried there. Although small-scale reliefs, with *putti*, were his speciality, Duquesnoy's study of Roman sculpture greatly influenced his work, and gave a heroic quality to his monumental statues. The sculptors from his studio, among them his younger brother Hieronymus and Artus Quellinus the Elder, were responsible to a large degree for a change of style in the southern Netherlands.

H. Gerson and E. H. ter Kuile   Art and Architecture in Belgium 1600-1800   London, 1960

St. Susanna, about 1633
Rome, S. Maria di Loreto

HIS WORKS INCLUDE

St. Andrew, 1633
Rome, St. Peter's
Monument to Bishop Anton Triest, about 1640-54
Ghent, Cath. of St. Bavon
Bacchanal
Rome, Gall. Borghese
Head of a Child
Stockholm, Nationalmus.

See also page 270

SIR ANTHONY VAN DYCK

1599-1641

The master of the full-length aristocratic portrait

Anthony van Dyck was born in Antwerp in 1599, one of the large family of a prosperous silk merchant. At the age of 11 he was apprenticed to Hendrik van Balen. It seems that from a very early age he had pupils of his own, and painted pictures whose merits were at once appreciated and highly valued. His first self-portrait, now in Vienna, is usually dated 1613 or 1614. By about 1620 he was being employed by Rubens, who seems to have trusted him to execute a large amount of work in parts of his vast pictures.

At the end of 1620 van Dyck was persuaded by the Earl of Arundel to go to London and enter the service of James I, but van Dyck remained there only a few months before being granted eight months leave. He did not return to England

Self-portrait
Munich, Alte Pin.

for 11 years. He traveled from Antwerp to Genoa, and except for a short interval he remained in Italy for the next five years. His sketchbook, now at Chatsworth, the home of the Dukes of Devonshire in Derbyshire, England, shows that van Dyck made an intense study of the Italian masters and particularly Titian. He conceived at this time the idea of the noble, full-length portrait, derived from Rubens but stylistically closer to Titian's work. The Genoese nobility supplied him with a number of sitters whose aristocratic bearing exactly suited his taste, and in Genoa today there are many portraits of the Genoese *haute noblesse* painted by van Dyck. The clothes, the backgrounds, the textures of rich silk and satins, the marble terraces and balustrades, all contributed to the courtly distinction of his work. Here too van Dyck began to paint those magnificent equestrian portraits, typically showing gray horses with flowing manes, and proud, handsome riders.

By the end of 1627 van Dyck was back in Antwerp, where he became the friendly rival of Rubens. Commissions poured in for every kind of work, portraits, historical pictures, religious scenes. In 1630 he was appointed painter to the Flemish court in conjunction with Rubens, and about this time he painted portraits of the Spanish Infanta, Maria de' Medici, and of Gaston d'Orléans and his wife, Margaret of Lorraine. His output was enormous, yet the pictures of this time show that his standard was extremely high and his craftmanship uniformly superb.

At the end of March, 1632, van Dyck returned to London where, apart from

Philippe Le Roy, Seigneur de Ravels,
1630
London, Wallace Coll.

The Lamentation, about 1634
Munich, Alte Pin.

brief visits to Antwerp and Paris, he remained until his death. Charles I of England and his queen, Henrietta Maria, showered honors on him. He painted numerous portraits of them and their courtiers. Van Dyck's plan for decorating the Banqueting Hall in Whitehall, for which Rubens painted the ceiling with scenes on the theme of War and Peace, was never carried out. Nevertheless the king gave van Dyck a handsome pension, a summer residence at Eltham Palace, a gold chain and medal, a knighthood in 1632, and an English bride, the daughter of Sir Patrick Ruthven.

Rubens died in 1640, and van Dyck thought of returning to his native Antwerp. He did go there for a short time and was asked to complete some work that Rubens had left unfinished. This he refused to do, and he returned to England. The last portraits he painted in England, of William II of Orange and Princess Mary, are now in Amsterdam. He died in his house in Blackfriars, London, in 1641 and was buried in the old St. Paul's Cathedral, London.

The Emperor Theodosius Refused Admission into the Church of St. Ambrose
London, N. G.

L. Cust *Anthony van Dyck* London, 1900
W. R. Valentenir   *The Art of the Low Countries* New York, 1914
*Introduction by W. R. Valentenir Catalogue of the Loan Exhibition of Fifty Paintings by A. van Dyck
    Detroit, 1929*
M. Whinney and O. Millar *English Art* Oxford, 1957

Charles I of England Hunting, about 1635
Paris, Louvre

Charles I of England on Horseback, about 1632
London, N. G.

41

A Belgian painter who became absorbed with masks and the macabre

The Lamp Boy, 1880
Brussels, Mus. Royaux des B-A.

HIS WORKS INCLUDE

The Expulsion from Paradise, 1887
Antwerp, Mus. Royal des B-A.
Ostend Harbor, 1890
Antwerp, Mus. Royal des B-A.
People in Masks Fighting over a
Hanged Man, 1891
Antwerp, Mus. Royal des B-A.
The Skate, 1892
Brussels, Mus. Royaux des B-A.

See also pages 201, 248, 249

L'Intrigue, 1890
Antwerp, Mus. Royal des B-A.

James Ensor was born on April 13, 1860, in Ostend, Belgium. His mother was Belgian, his father an English expatriate. The family's only source of income was a souvenir shop kept by Madame Ensor on the rue de Flandre in Ostend. Here she sold puppets, fans, china, objects made of seashells, and carnival masks —*bric-a-brac* that was to appear in startling guises in Ensor's work.

Ensor had only two years of formal schooling, begun when he was 13, but he started drawing and painting the countryside around Ostend at a very early age. He took lessons from two local watercolorists and, aged 17, entered the Brussels Academy. During his three years there he achieved a direct, simple, somber style, influenced to some extent by the French Impressionists and to a large degree by his own sensuous appreciation of textures. He frequently laid on his paint with a palette knife rather than a brush.

In 1880 Ensor returned to Ostend, where he lived for the rest of his life. At first he made numerous perceptive, unsentimental charcoal drawings of the local fishing community and painted portraits of his family and friends. In 1881 and 1882 he showed with various Brussels groups and at the Brussels and Paris Salons. With *Woman Eating Oysters*, 1882, his palette became brighter and more luminous. But this picture was refused by the Brussels groups and also by the Antwerp Salon. This was the first of many rejections that eventually made Ensor a bitter opponent of officialdom.

Ensor's art became the expression of a home life made unhappy by ill-feeling between his parents, and of his grudge against society in general. In the next few years he produced several canvases, such as *The Drunkards*, 1883, that depicted social outcasts. In 1884 he was a founder member of an *avant-garde* Brussels art society, Les XX, formed to oppose the established groups l'Essor and La Chrysalide. During its nine years of existence, 1884-93, Les XX played an important role in getting new, unnoticed painters, both French and Belgian, seen and recognized.

At Les XX's first exhibition Ensor exhibited his *Scandalized Masks*, 1883. This was the first of his compositions in which masks, used for purposes of symbolism and satire, were the dominant motif. Ensor's fascination with masks and the macabre, reflected in his illustrations to the stories of Edgar Allan Poe, were manifestations of the general taste for the strange and exotic prevalent in the late 19th century. In the 20th century his mask motif and its emotional overtones were adopted by Emil Nolde and the other artists of the German Expressionist movement, Die Brücke.

In 1886 Ensor made his first etchings, and began a series of Rembrandtesque drawings of the life of Christ that drew a parallel between the rejection of Christ and the rejection of his own art. This was most forcibly expressed in *The Entry of Christ into Brussels in 1889*, 1888. A huge canvas of about $8\frac{1}{2}$ by 14 feet, the brush strokes strong, the color apparently arbitrary, it was refused by Les XX and never placed on exhibition until the Ensor Show held in Brussels in 1929.

When Ensor could not count on showing his pictures even with Les XX, he was so discouraged that in 1893 he offered, without success, to sell for 8500 francs the contents of his studio. He thereafter exhibited only occasionally with the group, La Libre Esthétique, which replaced Les XX in 1893. Skeletons, like masks, became an obsessive theme, of which one of the most striking examples is *Skeletons Trying to Warm Themselves*, 1889. Ensor also painted a series of still-lifes of great vitality and rich coloring. He admired Antoine Watteau, Édouard Manet, and Joseph Mallord William Turner, and in turn influenced some of the German Expressionists and also Paul Klee, Marc Chagall, and the Surrealists.

Slowly Ensor was recognized. He held his first one-man show in Brussels in 1896, and three years later a retrospective exhibition in Paris. In the early years of the 20th century there were various Ensor exhibitions in Antwerp, Brussels, Paris, and New York. In 1903 Ensor was made a knight of the Order of Leopold, but by 1900 his best work was behind him. He spent the half-century remaining to him in reworking previous themes. He was created a baron in 1929 but the honor was based on earlier achievement. He stayed in Ostend through both World Wars, and died there on November 19, 1949, at the age of 89.

L. Tannenbaum   Ensor   New York, 1951
P. Hassaerts   Ensor   London, 1957

Woman Eating Oysters, 1882
Antwerp, Mus. Royal des B-A.

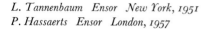

The Entry of Christ into Brussels in 1889, 1888
Antwerp, Mus. Royal des B-A., lent by Mrs. Louis Franck, London

Portrait of the Painter Paul Baignières
1894 *Brussels, Mus. Royaux des B-A.*

HENRI JACQUES ÉDOUARD EVENEPOEL 1872-1899

An artist who reacted against Impressionism

Henri Jacques Édouard Evenepoel was born in Nice, of Belgian parents, on October 3, 1872. His mother was staying on the Côte d'Azur in the hope of improving her health, but she died soon after Evenepoel was born. The family returned to Brussels in 1873. Evenepoel, a delicate child, was brought up by his grandparents on their estate near Brussels. He had every opportunity to become interested in painting, for his grandfather owned many paintings, and several of the family were painters. His first training took place in Brussels, in the studio of Blanc Garin, and in evening classes at the art school of Sint-Josse-ten-Noode. He also studied with the painter-decorator Adolphe Crespin.

In 1892 Evenepoel went to Paris, where he lived with a cousin. He studied decorative art at the École des Beaux-Arts, under Pierre Victor Galland, and then became a pupil of Gustave Moreau, who was an excellent teacher although he did not influence Evenepoel greatly. At this time he met Henri Matisse, with whom he

The Orange Market, about 1898 *Brussels, Mus. Royaux des B-A.*

44

made friends, and Georges Rouault. He admired Edgar Degas, but was more strongly influenced by Henri de Toulouse-Lautrec. He was also impressed by Édouard Manet's work, particularly *Olympia*, which he saw in the Luxembourg Palace.

Besides producing oil paintings, Evenepoel made many sketches of Paris life, and illustrated several of Edgar Allan Poe's stories, including "The Pit and the Pendulum" and "The Black Cat." He was especially interested in depicting life in the streets and in portraiture. In 1894 he exhibited *The Red Portrait* and three others in the Salon du Champ de Mars, with considerable success. Four years later he exhibited at the Cercle Artistique in Brussels, greatly perturbing the critics of the time.

During the winter of 1897-98 Evenepoel went to North Africa because of his ill-health. Algiers was a disappointment to him, but he was excited by the countryside, and the impact on his palette was immediate. He began to paint with a freer style, and with rich, luminous color. Unfortunately the visit did not improve his health, and he returned to Paris, where he died, aged 27, on December 27, 1899. Although he had had no time to develop his talent fully, he was among those who reacted against Impressionism, and he proved himself as a painter of the new aesthetic that was emerging in the last decades of the 19th century.

JAN VAN EYCK   about 1385-1441

A painter of immense technical skill who concentrated on color and light

Jan van Eyck was born probably in 1385. He was some 20 years the junior of his brother, Hubert. He became Hubert's working partner and with him closely studied the properties of colors. Though painting in oils was known before his day, he did much to improve the materials used and thus to produce the brilliance of color and durability of surface so notable in his work.

Hardly anything is known of the early life of the brothers, but in 1422 Jan, having left Hubert's workshop, became painter to John of Bavaria, Count of Holland, then living at The Hague. Three years later he entered the service of Philip the Good, Duke of Burgundy, for whom he undertook a variety of missions, some of them far removed from painting. Some were diplomatic, as in 1428, for instance, when he was a member of a mission sent to beg the hand of Philip's bride-to-be, the Infanta Isabella of Portugal.

Jan van Eyck married and settled in Bruges, where in 1431 he bought the house that was his home for the rest of his life. It was during the last ten years of his life that he produced most of the pictures upon which his immense reputation is founded. It has always been a problem to distinguish the work of one van Eyck brother from that of the other during the time they worked together, but Jan's later work is easily recognized. He had traveled in Spain and Portugal, and there had observed the effect of brilliant sunshine as well as the formations of rock and mountain—all so different from the comparative gloom and flatness of his native

Self-portrait, about 1433
London, N. G.

45

A Donor (detail): from the
Ghent Altarpiece, 1432
Ghent, Cath. of St. Bavon

land. Although too early to master the rules of perspective, Jan was the master of enchanting niceties of tone, of a variety of scenery, and of a minute perfection of finish.

The Adoration of the Holy Lamb, or the *Ghent Altarpiece*, is in the Cathedral of St. Bavon in Ghent, now reassembled there after many vicissitudes. It is the combined work of the van Eyck brothers, perhaps their most famous. It is about 23 feet high by 42 feet wide. An inscription on the outside, no doubt added later, states that it was begun by Hubert, "than whom was none greater," and finished by Jan in May, 1432. Critics differ as to the attribution of this or that part to one brother or the other, but they generally agree that the panels showing Adam and Eve and the portraits of the donors are the work of Jan van Eyck. The whole altarpiece is of

St. John the Evangelist (detail): from
the Ghent Altarpiece, 1432
Ghent, Cath. of St. Bavon

The Angel of the Annunciation:
from the Ghent Altarpiece, 1432
Ghent, Cath. of St. Bavon

The Virgin Annunciate:
from the Ghent Altarpiece, 1432
Ghent, Cath. of St. Bavon

particular interest as an early attempt to create a lifelike setting and atmosphere in a picture that is still in the tradition of sacred depiction and portraiture.

There are few works signed and dated by Jan van Eyck. The most familiar is the portrait, *Giovanni Arnolfini and his Wife*, 1434. This is the first picture to show two non-aristocratic people in their ordinary clothes and surroundings, and it is remarkable for its clear study of character and untroubled mastery of technique. The delightful small dog is as lovingly and observantly painted as his master and mistress.

Among the works usually attributed to Jan van Eyck are paintings now in the Gemäldegalerie, Dresden, the National Gallery in Washington, the National Gallery in Melbourne, the Louvre in Paris, and the Staatliche Museen in East and West Berlin. In some paintings an architectural background is skillfully included, and in all there is vivid color combined with a notable tenderness in general treatment. Common to many of the paintings, there is also an outstanding interest in the subleties of light playing on landscape.

Jan van Eyck had an immediate and important effect on painting, and his

The Pilgrims (detail): from the Ghent Altarpiece, 1432
Ghent, Cath. of St. Bavon

The Virgin, God the Son, and St. John the Baptist: from the Ghent Altarpiece, 1432
Ghent, Cath. of St. Bavon

The Angel Musicians: from the Ghent Altarpiece, 1432
Ghent, Cath. of St. Bavon

47

influence made itself more and more strongly felt, not only in the Netherlands, where he and Roger van der Weyden became the great protagonists of Netherlandish painting, but in every country north of the Alps. In the Arnolfini portrait alone Jan van Eyck brought an entirely original manifestation to the practice of his art. It is almost what became known later as a conversation piece, and when considered in relation to the works of his contemporaries, the freshness and directness of his vision is all the more remarkable.

W. H. J. Weale   Hubert and Jan Van Eyck: Their Life and Work   London, 1908
W. H. J. Weale and W. Brockwell   The Van Eycks and Their Art   London, 1912
M. Conway   The Van Eycks and Their Followers   London, 1912
L. van Puyvelde   The Holy Lamb   Brussels, 1947
L. Baldass   Jan van Eyck   London, 1952
M. W. Brockwell   The Van Eyck Problem   London, 1954

Portrait of a Man, 1432
London, N. G.

St. Elizabeth of Hungary (detail): from the Madonna and Child with Saints
New York, Frick Coll.

CAREL FABRITIUS   about 1622-1654

The finest of Rembrandt's pupils

Very little is known about the life of Carel Fabritius, even the date and place of his birth being uncertain. Some historians think he was born as early as 1614, but most consider the more likely date to have been about eight years later. The place was perhaps Midden-Beemster, near Amsterdam. What is certain is that he was killed in an explosion, probably of a powder magazine, in Delft on October 12, 1654. It is likely that many of his pictures were destroyed at the same time, because the entire list of his authentic works numbers only ten.

His father, a school-teacher who is said to have painted in his spare time, may well have been the first teacher of both Carel and his brother Barent, who was also a painter. In the early 1640's, probably in 1642, Carel studied painting in the studio of Rembrandt, his great contemporary, who was at the peak of his popular success. In 1650 Fabritius married a widow living in Delft, and in 1652 became a member of the Delft painters' guild. He was described by his widow as "painter to the Prince of Orange," but he seems to have been in financial difficulties shortly before his death in 1654.

The earliest known work by Fabritius is *The Raising of Lazarus*. His portrait of *Abraham de Potter*, in Amsterdam, dated 1640, is the work of a man who was already a masterly painter. A painting of a young man in Rotterdam, probably a self-portrait, was long thought to be the work of Rembrandt, until the signature of Fabritius was discovered.

The influence of his master was strong, and the earliest Fabritius pictures show it very clearly. Later it seems that he developed a style of his own. Whereas Rembrandt had made his portraits stand out from a dark background, Fabritius preferred to silhouette them against a light background. Moreover, he had an architectural turn of mind, and he is believed to have specialized in painting mural decorations with architectural features. None of this work survives, although it is sometimes believed that the delightful *trompe l'oeil* painting, *The Goldfinch*, 1654, was part of such a decoration.

There is no doubt, even with only ten pictures on which to form a judgment, that Fabritius was a very accomplished and notable painter in his own right. *Musical Instrument Dealer with a View of Delft*, 1652, is quite unlike any other Dutch painting of the period. Fabritius seems to have been interested in problems of optics and in the use of mirrors in his paintings. This possibility becomes the more interesting when it is remembered that Vermeer, said to have been his pupil, used mirrors in several of his most famous pictures.

N. Maclaren   The Dutch School, N. G. Catalogue   London, 1960

The Goldfinch, 1654
The Hague, Mauritshuis

Musical Instrument Dealer with a View of Delft (detail) 1652
London, N. G.

Portrait of a Young Man
Munich, Alte Pin.

CORNELIS FLORIS

A sculptor with a highly decorative style

Façade (detail) 1561-66
Antwerp, Town Hall

HIS WORKS INCLUDE

Tabernacle, about 1550
Zoutleeuw, Belgium, Church
Town Hall, 1561-66
Antwerp
Rood-screen and Rood-loft, 1572
Tournai, Belgium, Cathedral

See also page 265

Cornelis Floris was born in Antwerp in 1514. He was a painter of initials and a draftsman for engravings before turning to sculpture. In 1539 he became a master in the painters' guild, and shortly afterwards went to Italy. By 1549, however, he was back in Antwerp, for he was recorded as the dean of the guild in that year. In the same year he contributed to the decorations devised for the entry of Philip II into the town, and through the help of a friend he obtained a commission for some sepulchral monuments for Königsberg in Prussia. During 1546 and 1547 he had designed some grotesque initials for the guild book, and he later published books with engravings of decorative forms.

Floris began his career as a sculptor and an architect in 1549. He carved five plaques for the Great Church in Breda between that year and 1555. Among his most important monuments was the tomb of Frederik I of Denmark, begun in 1550 and finished two years later. This was designed in a pure Renaissance style, and was not as ornate as many Flemish monuments. Floris became the head of a large and prosperous workshop that turned out work of a uniformly high quality, though little of it can be attributed to the hand of the master himself. He made many monuments and plaques for tombs, reliefs and decorations for buildings, and tabernacles for churches.

Antwerp Town Hall was designed by Floris, and became the model after which other town halls were built. Much architectural work is attributed to him on stylistic grounds, but there is little documentary evidence of his numerous activities. He executed a number of architectural decorations in Tournai Cathedral, which included the rood-loft, and many relief medallions representing the Passion. Floris was buried in Antwerp in October, 1575.

H. Gerson and E. H. ter Kuile   Art and Architecture in Belgium 1600-1800   London, 1960

HIS WORKS INCLUDE

Still-life with Game, 1651
Stockholm, Nationalmus.
Wolves Attacked by Dogs, 1652
Oslo, Nasjonalgall.
Still-life with Boar's Head
Vienna, Kunsthist. Mus.
Swans Frightened by Dogs
Antwerp, Mus. Royal des B-A.

See also page 182

JAN FYT

A painter of still-lifes

Jan Fyt was born in Antwerp in 1611, the son of a leading merchant. He attended the studio of Frans Snyders, who influenced his choice of subject-matter, which was mainly animals and sporting still-lifes with game. He also produced some flower paintings and scenes with horses, but landscapes by Fyt are rare.

In 1630 Fyt became a master in the painters' guild of Antwerp, and the next year he journeyed to Rome by way of Paris. In Rome he joined the band of Dutch and Flemish painters called the "Bentveughels" or the "Flock of Birds." He was given the nickname "Goudvink" (Goldfinch). He became very popular and had many pupils working in his studio. From 1645 his style grew increasingly independent of Snyders' and he acquired greater dexterity. He developed a free, Baroque manner, painting with glazes and with dashes of color.

Fyt's work reached its climax in 1650 when he achieved his richest coloring, strongest form, and most striking contrasts of light and shade. In these qualities he surpassed his teacher Snyders. Some of the figures in his paintings are by Jan Erasmus Quellinus and Theodor van Thulden. He died in 1661.

H. Gerson and E. H. ter Kuile   Art and Architecture in Belgium 1600-1800   London, 1960

Still-life with Page (detail) 1644
London, Wallace Coll.

Wolf (detail)
Edinburgh, N. G. of Scotland

GEERTGEN TOT SINT JANS

active late 15th century

A gifted painter of original light effects

Geertgen tot Sint Jans, whose name means "Little Gerard of the Brethren of St. John," was born in Leiden probably about 1467. A pupil of Albert van Ouwater, he was appointed official painter to the Order of the Knights of St. John in Haarlem.

From among the works attributed to Geertgen, the most certain are two large panels, originally the back and front of a single panel, from an altarpiece in the Monastery of St. John in Haarlem. They are *The Lamentation over the Dead Christ* and *Julian the Apostate Burning the Bones of St. John the Baptist*. The strange egg-

HIS WORKS INCLUDE

The Raising of Lazarus, about 1480
Paris, Louvre
The Adoration of the Magi
Amsterdam, Rijksmus.
The Martyrdom of St. Lucy
Amsterdam, Rijksmus.
The Tree of Jesse
Amsterdam, Rijksmus.

See also page 140

shaped heads in these pictures have caused a group of works to be attributed to Geertgen, but many of these show puzzling inconsistencies of style. One of the best known is a *Nativity* in which the atmosphere is realistically nocturnal, one of the earliest instances in northern painting, but which has the delightful innovation of having light emanating from the Child Himself. The simplified composition and the use of a single source of light were to be more fully explored by the 17th-century French painter Georges de La Tour.

Geertgen, perhaps the most gifted painter of the northern Netherlands at this time, died in Haarlem about 1495. He is believed to have been only 28 years old.

The Nativity, at Night, early work
London, N. G.

Julian the Apostate Burning the Bones of St. John the Baptist, middle period
Vienna, Kunsthist. Mus.

The Virgin in Glory, about 1490
Rotterdam, Boymans-van Beuningen

JOOS VAN GHENT   active 1460 - after 1475

The only Netherlandish painter recorded in Urbino

Joos van Ghent, also known as Justus of Ghent, possibly the same person as Joos van Wassenhove, was one of the painters who, by working abroad, helped to make Flemish art respected throughout Europe in the 15th century. In 1460 he became a master in the Antwerp painters' guild, and four years later in the guild at Ghent. There he met Hugo van der Goes, who was probably still an apprentice. By 1473 he had emigrated to Italy, where he stayed for the rest of his life. He worked for a while as court painter to Duke Federico da Montefeltro in Urbino, collaborating on various paintings with Pedro Berruguete and Piero della Francesca, and executing the celebrated series of *Twenty-eight Famous Men*, which was once wrongly ascribed to Berruguete. In 1475 he went to Rome, and nothing more is known of his movements.

Van Ghent's figures never lost their solemn Flemish angularity, but by blending them with rich Italian Renaissance settings, the painter during his own lifetime acquired a reputation for originality of composition.

E. G. Troche   Painting in the Netherlands in the 15th and 16th Centuries   London, 1936

HIS WORKS INCLUDE

Triptych of the Crucifixion, 1464
Ghent, Cath. of St. Bavon

Twenty-eight Famous Men,
about 1474
*Paris, Louvre;
Urbino, Ducal Pal. Gall. of the Marches*

See also page 138

Triptych of The Crucifixion, 1464
Ghent, Cath. of St. Bavon

Federico da Montefeltro, his Sons and Members of his Court (detail)
London, Royal Coll.

JAKOB DE GHEYN I   about 1532-1582

A versatile craftsman famous for his drawings and glass painting

Little is known about the life of Jakob de Gheyn I, but he appears to have been born in a ship on the Zuider Zee about 1532. In 1558 de Gheyn was a member of the Antwerp painters' guild. He was a craftsman who could turn his hand to work in various mediums, though he probably was most active as a glass painter. He made numerous windows for churches in Amsterdam and Antwerp, including the windows in St. Walburga Church. He was commissioned by the Italian community in Utrecht to design some windows, which were executed in 1580.

In addition to his work on church windows, de Gheyn painted miniatures and portraits and made drawings for engravings. His most notable work was *The Demolition of the Spanish Citadel in Antwerp in 1577*, a subject painted by several artists. He died, probably in Utrecht in 1582, leaving some windows unfinished. His son, the better-known Jakob de Gheyn II, also became a painter and draftsman and was influenced by his father's work.

HIS WORKS INCLUDE

The Demolition of the Spanish Citadel in Antwerp in 1577
(recorded by an engraving)

Studies of Mice
Amsterdam, Rijksmus.

See also page 218

White Spanish Stallion of
Prince Maurice, about 1603
Amsterdam, Rijksmus.

HIS WORKS INCLUDE

Flowerpiece, 1612
The Hague, Gemeentemus.
Venus and Cupid
Amsterdam, Rijksmus.

See also page 222

JAKOB DE GHEYN II   1565-1629

A celebrated engraver and painter of flowerpieces

Jakob de Gheyn II, born in Antwerp in 1565, first followed his father's profession of glass painting. He then became a pupil of the Dutch engraver Hendrik Goltzius, working with him in Haarlem from 1585 to 1587. His choice of master was largely dictated by his conversion to the Protestant faith, which led him to leave Antwerp at the age of 20.

By 1591 de Gheyn had a high reputation for the quality of his engravings, and in that year he was invited by the Jesuits of Antwerp to return there and engrave the plates for an important book. He declined and instead went to Amsterdam, where he became a master of the painters' guild and was one of the actors in a play given in honor of Prince Maurice in 1594. A year later he married into the aristocracy of The Hague.

After some time spent working in Leiden, de Gheyn settled at The Hague, where he designed gardens for the stadtholder's palace. Until about 1603 he was chiefly active as an engraver of portraits and compositions by himself and by other artists. In 1606 he was commissioned to paint a flowerpiece to be given to Maria de' Medici, and Emperor Rudolph II bought one of his flower paintings. De Gheyn later produced a book with miniature paintings of flowers and insects, which the emperor also bought. De Gheyn died at The Hague at the age of 64.

Portrait of a Man
*New York, Met. Mus. Bequest of Mrs.
Havermeyer, 1929, The H. O. Havermeyer
Coll.*

HUGO VAN DER GOES   about 1440-1482

The painter of the Portinari Altarpiece

Hugo van der Goes was born probably about 1440 in Ghent, where he chiefly worked. In 1467 he was enrolled in the painters' guild of Ghent, and undertook the many and varied jobs usual for an artist of that time. He painted the papal escutcheon over the town gates, designed the windows in St. John's Church and, with Hans Memling and Dieric Bouts, painted wall-hangings and decorations for the marriage of Charles the Bold and Margaret of York in Bruges in 1468.

In 1473 van der Goes was made dean of the guild and received a commission from Tommaso Portinari for the famous altarpiece, now in the Uffizi in Florence. The dramatic design demonstrates a mastery of large composition unusual among Flemish artists. The intricate pattern of the distant landscape is contrasted with the massed figures in the foreground, a delicately drawn hand or piece of embroidery is set against a dark cloak or book, and the whole forms a flat patchwork style of painting that was soon to be superseded by the 16th-century emphasis on chiaroscuro. This altarpiece was shipped straight to Italy and so had no influence on the mainstream of Netherlandish painting.

In 1475 van der Goes became a lay brother in the Augustinian monastery of Rode Klooster near Brussels. He continued to paint and to receive visitors, one of whom was Emperor Maximilian. He traveled occasionally—once to Louvain to value the estate of Dieric Bouts, and in 1479 to Cologne. In Cologne he is said to have had an attack of religious melancholia, which recurred intermittently until his death in 1482.

E. G. Troche Painting in the Netherlands in the 15th and 16th Centuries London, 1936

HIS WORKS INCLUDE

The Original Sin, 1468
Vienna, Kunsthist. Mus.
Trinity Altarpiece, about 1479
Edinburgh, N. G. of Scotland
The Holy Family with St. Anne and a Donor
Brussels, Mus. Royaux des B-A.

See also pages 135, 211

St. Anthony, St. Matthew, and Donor: left panel from the Portinari Altarpiece, about 1476
Florence, Uffizi

St. Mary Magdalen, St. Margaret, and Lady Donor: right panel from the Portinari Altarpiece, about 1476
Florence, Uffizi

The Angel Gabriel: exterior panel from the Portinari Altarpiece, about 1476
Florence, Uffizi

VINCENT VAN GOGH   1853-1890

A Post-Impressionist painter and precursor of Expressionism

Vincent van Gogh was born in Zundert, in the Dutch province of Brabant, in 1853. He was the eldest son of a church minister, and felt from an early age that he should make preaching his life's work. But he also began drawing. On his first visit to London at the age of 20, and also when he returned to England as a lay preacher three years later, he sent back drawings to his parents.

Meanwhile he visited Paris in 1874 and returned there the next year to work at the Goupil Gallery, of which his uncle was a director. After a short time he quarreled with the management and left. He then began his studies for the ministry, but failed to pass his examinations. Instead, late in 1878, he went to work as a lay

Self-portrait with Bandaged Ear, 1889
London, Courtauld Inst. Gall.

Thatched Roofs, 1884
London, Tate

Study for The Potato Eaters, 1885
Otterlo, Holland, Kröller-Müller

The Reaper (after J. F. Millet) 1889
Amsterdam, Stedelijk Mus.

preacher among the miners of the Borinage in Belgium. He was soon dismissed as unsuitable.

From this succession of disappointments van Gogh turned, at the age of 27, to art, staying on for a time in the Borinage. In October, 1880, he made his way to Brussels, where he took a short course at the Brussels Academy. He then went back to his parents in Etten, Holland. Some months later his disputes with them became insupportable and he went to The Hague. There he studied under a relative of his, the painter Anton Mauve. He spent the last three months of 1883 in the desolate countryside of Drenthe near the Dutch-German border, returning at the end of December to his parents, now in Nuenen.

Jean François Millet and Joseph Israels were the artists whom van Gogh most admired and copied. Like Millet he reproduced the life of the workers around him, creating an enormous output of studies of the miners of the Borinage, the poor of the almshouses and workhouse of The Hague, the landscapes and peasants of Drenthe and Nuenen. Van Gogh's most important work of this period was *The Potato Eaters*, 1885, a Millet-type painting with a strong sacramental quality. Although his compositions were careful, it was the content of a picture that always took first place in his eyes. Interested in any artist with a social message to convey, he made a collection of English magazine illustrations. An emotional influence of a different sort in these years was his deep and unrequited attachment to his cousin Kee Vos-Stricker, a young widow with a small son.

Van Gogh began to be aware of the existence of Impressionism. He knew nothing about it, though he was interested in the color theories of Delacroix. He learned the better to appreciate these through his contact, on a short visit to Antwerp, early in 1886, with the work of Rubens. During this visit, though living in extreme poverty, he discovered and began collecting Japanese prints. Touches of lighter pigment started to enliven the dark, heavy coloring of his earlier paintings. At the Antwerp Academy he learned nothing, since he refused to compromise with the professors over his forthright approach to drawing.

In February, 1886, he left Antwerp for Paris, where he stayed for two years, a critical period in his development. At last he was able to judge Impressionism for himself and to meet its exponents. He saw their work, and that of Camille Corot and Honoré Daumier, at the Goupil Gallery, where his brother Theo, an ardent and generous supporter of the Impressionists, worked. Henri de Toulouse-Lautrec painted van Gogh's portrait. Camille Pissarro enthusiastically explained pointillism to him. The art shop proprietor Père Tanguy let him have paints and canvas in exchange for his work. He also met Edgar Degas and Georges Seurat and became friends with Paul Signac, Paul Gauguin and, in 1887, Émile Bernard.

Van Gogh spent hours in the Louvre and studied figure drawing with Fernand Cormon. But it was as he came to appreciate Impressionism that his color intensified and his handling grew freer. Living in Paris with Theo, his constant support to the end of his life, he painted flower studies, still-lifes, and landscapes. He gradually developed a pointillist, or neo-impressionist technique, but without approaching it scientifically as Signac and Seurat. In 1887 paintings by van Gogh were hung at the offices of "La Revue Indépendante," the restaurant La Fourche, and the lobby of the Théâtre Libre. He also organized an exhibition of his own work, and that of Bernard, Toulouse-Lautrec, and Louis Anquetin, at the cabaret Le Tambourin.

Life in Paris began to affect van Gogh's health. Suffering from depression, he took to heavy drinking. In any case he was too excitable for his brother to find it easy to live with him. In February, 1888, he left for Arles in Provence.

The south of France was as much a revelation to him as Paris had been. He worked in a frenzy, living alone as cheaply as possible and eating very little. Color and strong sunlight filtered into his painting, as he searched for a simpler, more powerful line and greater expression, through color, of moods and feelings. The necessity and the problems of color symbolism preoccupied him. At this time he painted the *Night Café*, to him "a place where one can ruin oneself, go mad, or commit a crime."

Meanwhile Provence became for him the equivalent of Japan. He looked for Japanese motifs. A drawbridge, for example, or an orchard, recurs time and again in his work of this period. So do the "series," which he painted as parallels to the "series that occur in Japanese prints." He made many drawings in pen and ink and experimented with textures of paint. He planned an artists' colony in the south of France in letters to Theo, Gauguin, and Bernard. With Gauguin and Bernard he exchanged self-portraits in the Japanese custom. Portraiture began to assume great importance for him.

In September, 1888, having made up his mind that Gauguin should come south,

A Garden at St. Rémy, 1889
London, Tate

View at Auvers, 1890
London, Tate

57

The Pipe on the Chair, 1889
London, Tate

Landscape with Cypress Trees, 1889
London, Tate

van Gogh moved into the Yellow House in Arles. Gauguin left Brittany with reluctance and joined him there in October. He did not like Provence. Soon tensions arose between the two painters. Gauguin's method of working from memory irritated van Gogh. There were clashes and heated arguments. By December, when they visited Montpellier to see paintings by Delacroix and Gustave Courbet in the local museum, Gauguin was already thinking of returning to the north. This, and the news that Theo was engaged to be married, upset van Gogh. On December 24, 1888, he had his first mental seizure. Gauguin claimed afterward that it was because van Gogh threatened him that he spent the night in a hotel. That evening, in any case, van Gogh cut off part of his own ear, to offer it to the prostitutes of the local brothel. He was taken to hospital, where he lay unconscious for three days.

From this time on, life became increasingly difficult for van Gogh. He suffered more frequent seizures, which eventually so perturbed him that, hoping to be cured and to avoid being a burden on the recently married Theo, he entered the Saint-Rémy asylum of his own free will. Periods of mental clarity alternated with his attacks, so that he was able to produce many paintings and drawings both inside and outside the asylum grounds. He worked in a changed style, frenzied and turbulent, with cypress trees a persistent motif. To calm himself, he made many copies after Delacroix, Daumier, Rembrandt, and his consistent favorite, Millet. Although his tentative suggestion of joining Gauguin in Brittany was not encouraged, he was determined to return to the north of France.

In January, 1890, some of van Gogh's paintings were exhibited in Brussels with Les XX. An article on him appeared in "Mercure de France." In March, 1890, ten of his pictures were hung at the Salon des Indépendants in Paris, and highly praised. In May he was able to leave Saint-Rémy, pay a short visit to Paris to see Theo and his family, and settle at Auvers-sur-Oise under the watchful eye of Dr. Gachet, a friend of Pissarro and an amateur painter and collector. At first van Gogh painted with great determination in the surrounding countryside. Soon, worried about his brother's problems and his own chances of recovery, his depression returned and he quarreled with Dr. Gachet. His last turbulent paintings were of wheatfields. On July 27 he shot himself. Theo came down from Paris, and on July 29, 1890, Vincent van Gogh died. Within a few years his paintings were as widely influential as any produced in his generation. The French Fauvists and the German Expressionists were deeply indebted to him.

M. Schapiro   Van Gogh   New York, 1950
C. Nordenfalk   Van Gogh   London, 1953
D. Cooper   Drawings and Watercolors by Van Gogh   London, 1955
V. van Gogh   The Complete Collected Letters   New York, 1958

HENDRIK GOLTZIUS

A Dutch painter, engraver, and draftsman

Hendrik Goltzius was born in 1558 in Mulbrecht, near Venlo in the Netherlands, and probably began to study art with his father, who was a glass painter. Later he became a pupil of Dirck Volckertsz Coornhert. In about 1577 the Goltzius family moved to Haarlem.

Goltzius very quickly established a reputation with his engraving, and before the 1580's he was among the most popular of the Dutch artists who worked in this medium. During this time Haarlem, with Utrecht, was a center of the Mannerist style in the Netherlands, in which varied elements of Italian and native art were mingled. Goltzius was among those who came into direct contact with late 16th-century Italian art, for in 1590 he visited Italy, traveling all over the country. He stayed in Florence, Venice, Naples, and Rome, taking particular interest in the sculpture and making numerous sketches of it.

Goltzius returned to the Netherlands in 1591, and about this time he made a journey in the company of the painter and writer Karel van Mander and Cornelis Cornelisz. After this trip the three men set up an "academy" in Haarlem. The principal subject was the study of the nude, with instruction in contemporary Italian artistic theory. The students of this school became the nucleus of the academic movement in Haarlem.

Late in his career, probably about 1600, Goltzius no longer limited himself to drawings and prints, but began to produce oil paintings in which his interest in Italian art was evident. He drew his subject-matter almost entirely from classical mythology, and his use of color owed much to his study of Venetian painting. His work greatly influenced the French engraver Claude Mellan.

K. van Mander *Het Schilderboek* Haarlem, 1604 (English translation in C. van der Wall *Dutch and Flemish Painters* New York, 1936)

Mercury, 1611
Haarlem, Frans Hals Mus.

HIS WORKS INCLUDE

Titus Bound to the Rock, 1613
Haarlem, Frans Hals Mus.
Pomone and Vertumne Transformed into Old Women
Amsterdam, Rijksmus.
Hercules and Cacus
Haarlem, Frans Hals Mus.
Minerva
Haarlem, Frans Hals Mus.

See also page 220

JAN VAN GOYEN

A founder of the Dutch landscape school

Jan van Goyen, one of the earliest Dutch landscape painters, is important as one of the founders of a school of painting that produced many outstanding artists. He was born in Leiden and studied under various masters. In 1615 he went to France. Back in Haarlem he was influenced by Esaias van de Velde, one of the exponents of a renewed vision of nature. Up to the time of van de Velde, Dutch art had preserved a tradition of minute scale, first in the style of Pieter Bruegel the Elder, and later, retaining vivid color but with more accent on local motifs. In 1618 van Goyen returned to Leiden, and he seems to have moved to The Hague about 1640.

Van Goyen was evidently a man of great importance in his own time, and so had

Windmill by a River (detail) 1642
London, N. G.

River Scene with Fishing Boats, 1638
London, N. G.

HIS WORKS INCLUDE

Winter Landscape with Skaters, 1619
Brussels, Mus. Royaux des B-A.

River Estuary, 1639
Norwich, England, Castle Mus.

Scheveningen, 1644
London, N. G.

Riverscape with a Castle in the
Distance, 1652
Rouen, Mus. des B-A.

See also pages 184, 235

opportunities to watch the developments taking place around him. He is said to have given guidance to Salomon van Ruysdael and Pieter Potter, and he was a friend of Anthony van Dyck, who painted his portrait. Rembrandt noticed his work, and one of van Goyen's daughters married Jan Steen. He once received a commission from the stadtholder Frederik Hendrik, and he executed one commission for the municipality of The Hague. These are his only known commissions.

Van Goyen's pictures are in the prevalent style of small-scale landscapes, meticulously painted and used as a background for the scenes of village life so dear to Dutch painting. Until 1625 this remained typical of van Goyen's art. He then began to work on a larger scale. His work tended to be executed almost in monochrome, but the light and shade of river scenes came to grip his imagination. He concentrated on houses near water and ships lying on the river and canals, and he had his greatest success and became best known in this field. He also painted ice-scenes with sleds and skaters, and he had a remarkable feeling for cloudy skies. His importance lies in his lyrical interpretation of landscapes in a very personal manner, based on the numerous sketches and drawings he made out-of-doors. His pictures were always painted in his studio.

Van Goyen died in 1656. If not among the greatest of Dutch landscape artists, he was certainly one of the innovators, and he had considerable influence on his young contemporaries. His significance in the development of Dutch landscape painting was rediscovered at the beginning of the 20th century.

Admiral Sir L. G. Preston   Sea and River Painters in the 17th Century   London, 1937
N. Maclaren   The Dutch School, N. G. Catalogue   London, 1960

A River Scene with Fishermen
Laying a Net (detail)
London, N. G.

Landscape, about 1645
West Berlin, Staatl. Mus.

GABRIEL GRUPELLO

1644-1730

A decorative sculptor

Gabriel Grupello was born on May 23, 1644, the son of an artillery captain in the service of the Spanish. He was apprenticed to Artus Quellinus the Younger, and became a master in Brussels in 1674. He was later appointed sculptor to Charles II of Spain and also to the city of Brussels.

In 1675 Grupello carved a marble fountain for the Fishmongers' Guild. The following year he executed a monument commissioned by the widowed Comtesse de La Tour et Tassis to commemorate her husband. Placed in the Church of Notre Dame du Sablon in Brussels, it includes a decorative figure of *Faith*. Because of the scarcity of commissions, Grupello emigrated to Germany in 1695. He went to Düsseldorf and entered the service of the Elector Johan Wilhelm, who appointed him court sculptor. Grupello married there in 1698. In 1711 he completed a large equestrian statue of the elector, which was placed in the main square of Düsseldorf. He carved a number of crosses in ivory, one of which remains in the Imperial Treasury in Vienna. A cross in Aachen Cathedral was probably also made by him.

Later Grupello returned to the Netherlands. He went first to Brussels and then on to Aachen in Germany. He died in 1730. His work was notable for its strength, form, and decorative qualities.

H. Gerson and E. H. ter Kuile   Art and Architecture in Belgium 1600-1800   London, 1960

Samson and Delilah
West Berlin, Staatl. Mus.

HIS WORKS INCLUDE

Fountain for the Fishmongers' Guild, 1675   *Brussels, Mus. Royaux des B-A.*
Faith, 1676
Brussels, Notre Dame du Sablon
Diana
Brussels, Mus. Royaux des B-A.
Narcissus
Brussels, Mus. Royaux des B-A.

See also page 275

FRANS HALS

about 1585-1666

A master of the group portrait

Frans Hals was born in Antwerp, sometime in the troubled mid-1580's. When he was still very young his parents moved to Haarlem.

Little is known of the first part of Hals's life. His earliest important works seem to have been *The Banquet of the Officers of the Arquebusiers of St. George* and *Two Boys Playing and Singing*, both dated 1616. At this time, when he was in his thirties, he seems again to have been in Antwerp. Between 1600 and 1603 he worked in the public studio of Karel van Mander in Haarlem. He married about 1610, and the birth of a son was recorded a year later. His wife died in 1615, and he married again in 1617. He worked hard and successfully enough to support a family of ten children, although he was to relapse into a period of disillusion and poverty before his death in 1666.

Hals's first period of free, nearly impressionistic brushwork developed about 1625, reaching a peak in 1627 with a second group portrait of *The Arquebusiers of St. George*. This work demonstrates his distinctive qualities. Pre-eminent among these is his skill in composing an interesting group in which each individual is

The Laughing Cavalier, 1624
London, Wallace Coll.

f Hals

The Gypsy Woman, 1630
Paris, Louvre

HIS WORKS INCLUDE

Portrait of Jakobus Zaffius, 1611
Haarlem, Frans Hals Mus.

Yonker Ramp and his Sweetheart,
1623
New York, Met. Mus.

Daniel van Aeken Playing the Fiddle,
about 1630
Stockholm, Nationalmus.

Portrait of a Woman with a Fan,
London, N. G.

Portrait of a Man, 1643
New York, Met. Mus.

See also pages 160, 161, 226

given equal attention. This was very necessary to his success, for it was the fashion of the time that each member of the guild or company should pay an equal share of the cost of the work, and therefore each member expected to have the same importance in the composition. Apart from this quality, Hals possessed an extraordinary facility in catching character and expression, and a virtuoso technique in the rendering of silk, velvet, starched linen, and especially flesh. In his heyday Hals had a large workshop. As many as 20 versions of some of his pictures exist. His pupils included Adriaen Brouwer and Adriaen van Ostade.

After 1640, Hals's second period developed with a striking change of color and a new dignity imparted to the sitters. Black and subtle grays dominated, relieved only by the flesh tints, which were increasingly restrained. This change was perhaps due to the proximity of Rembrandt's work in Amsterdam.

There were a few significant achievements at the end of Hals's life. The last portrait groups, the striking *Lady Governors of the Old Men's Home at Haarlem*, 1664, and its companion, *Governors of the Old Men's Home at Haarlem*, are masterpieces in an almost monochromatic palette. Eventually Hals dispensed altogether with the use of underpainting, applying his oils directly to the bare canvas. It is arguable whether in the limitations of his virtuosity Hals achieved the true mark of greatness. Certainly the restriction of his later years revealed the critical vision of a wiser man who was able to concentrate on the essentials of the visual world.

G. S. Davies   Frans Hals   London, 1902
W. R. Valentenir   Frans Hals' Paintings in America   Westport, Conn., 1936
W. S. Trivas   The Paintings of Frans Hals   New York, 1941
N. Maclaren   The Dutch School, N. G. Catalogue   London, 1960

The Banquet of the Officers of the
Arquebusiers of St. George (detail)
1616   *Haarlem, Frans Hals Mus.*

The Banquet of the Officers of the St. Hadrian Militia Company, 1633
Haarlem, Frans Hals Mus.

MEINDERT HOBBEMA

1638-1709

A landscape painter of the second half of the 17th century

Meindert Hobbema was born in 1638, probably in Amsterdam, where he seems to have lived all his life. Jakob van Ruisdael was his friend and for about two years, from 1655 to 1657, his instructor. Ruisdael witnessed Hobbema's marriage in 1668, and often shared painting expeditions with him. They frequently painted the same view, as for instance *The Ruins of Brederode Castle*, 1671.

Hobbema can be classed among the most skillful and powerful of Dutch landscape painters, with a love for the light and play of sunshine that was not shared by many of his contemporaries. The countryside, with its trees, churches, and farms, was his favorite subject. *The Avenue at Middelharnis* is one of the most famous landscape paintings in the world.

Hobbema was by no means an industrious painter, and seems almost to have ceased work after his marriage. Through his wife's influence, he was given employment in the imported wine trade and spent his time estimating the contents of casks. Nearly all Hobbema's pictures are earlier than 1670, though the famous *Avenue* is dated 1689. For a long time there was some doubt about this date, and it was generally thought to have been 1669. Internal evidence, however, connected with the known dates at which the trees were planted and the date the beacon at the harbor entrance was raised, seem to make it certain that 1689 is the correct date. It is curious that a man who had almost ceased painting by 1670 should have produced this solitary masterpiece, distinguished by as superb an artistry as anything in his youth, after an interval of nearly 20 years.

Hobbema was apparently unsuccessful in selling his pictures, for he died a poor man and was buried in the paupers' section of an Amsterdam cemetery. Nearly 200 of his pictures are known. He was much admired by collectors, especially in England, and by the painters of the English landscape school.

N. Maclaren   The Dutch School, N. G. Catalogue   London, 1960

HIS WORKS INCLUDE

Cottages in a Wood, 1660
London, N. G.

Stream by a Wood, 1664
London, N. G.

Country Land, about 1665
West Berlin, Staatl. Mus.

Entrance to a Village, about 1665
New York, Met. Mus.

Road Winding past Cottages
in a Wood, about 1668
London, N. G.

See also page 188

Landscape (detail) about 1670
London, N. G.

Watermill, about 1670
London, N. G.

The Ruins of Brederode Castle, 1671
London, N. G.

Courtyard of a House in Delft, 1658
London, N. G.

The painter of Dutch courtyards

Very little is known of Pieter de Hooch's earlier years, except that he was born in Rotterdam in 1629, perhaps the son of a butcher. By 1653 he was certainly employed by a rich merchant, Justus de la Grange, in one of those varied capacities that seem to have been quite usual at the time, his post being that of "painter and manservant."

In 1654 de Hooch married a girl from Delft, and in 1655 the artist in him had so far eclipsed the manservant as to allow him to become a member of the Delft painters' guild. It was here that he painted most of the pictures that have since made his great reputation. Carel Fabritius (killed by an explosion in 1654) and Jan Vermeer were both working at Delft, and it is not surprising that de Hooch seems to have been stimulated by Vermeer's influence. He was not, however, Vermeer's follower, but he tried to be his equal.

So far as his career is concerned, de Hooch seems to have stayed on in Delft for some years, but there is nothing definite known of his life until about 1667, when he was in Amsterdam. By then he was only 37 years old, but his work from about 1670 onwards was of far less distinction than that of his twenties. He seems to have been moving in a rather more aristocratic society, with the result that his pictures lost in feeling as they increased in elegance. He died about 1684.

Man with Dead Birds and Other Figures in a Stable, early work
London, N. G.

Interior, about 1658
London, N. G.

64

It is inevitable that the work of de Hooch should be closely compared with that of Vermeer. They were almost the same age—Vermeer was two years and some months the younger—and they were working in Delft at the same time. Moreover, they painted pictures of a similar type, both being masters of the Dutch interior and both possessing a particular and loving eye for the effects of sunlight and the texture of fabrics and furniture.

De Hooch is thought to have painted only one large picture, destroyed by fire in Rotterdam in 1864. He is most familiar as the painter of the domestic scene in a typical Dutch courtyard. In his early years de Hooch was evidently intrigued by the jollities of the life around him, with soldiers and their girls, with stables and horses, with cavaliers and their ladies dining and dancing. Such subjects gave him the opportunity to treat two different themes in the same painting.

First is the human element; the maid at work cleaning the yard, watched by her mistress, for example, and second, as a background to the human element, a studied design of Dutch domestic architecture. The corner of a building fits into the scene, and perhaps an open door in the middle distance gives a view of a more distant part of the yard. Although his paintings are on a small scale, their colors are still as warm and bright as on the day they were first applied.

N. Maclaren   The Dutch School, N. G. Catalogue   London, 1960
W. R. Valentenir   Pieter de Hooch   New York, n. d.

Maternal Bliss, about 1675
Amsterdam, Rijksmus.

HIS WORKS INCLUDE

Dutch Courtyard, about 1656
Washington, D. C., N. G., Mellon Coll.
Card Players, 1658
London, Royal Coll.
The Linen Cupboard, 1663
Amsterdam, Rijksmus.
Woman at a Window Reading
a Letter, 1664
Budapest, Mus. of Fine Arts
Musical Party in a Courtyard, 1677
London, N. G.

See also page 176

JAN JOSEF HOREMANS the ELDER   1682-1759

A painter of genre scenes

Jan Josef Horemans the Elder, born in Antwerp in 1682, was one of the most important representatives of a famous family of painters in the 17th century. In 1694 he became the pupil of the sculptor Michel Vervoort, and later entered the studio of a genre painter.

About 1707 Horemans became a master in the painters' guild of Antwerp. He painted scenes from the lives of the aristocrats of Antwerp in the style of the Dutch painters Jan Steen and Adriaen van Ostade, as well as such genre subjects as sick men, people making music, alchemists, scholars, and card players.

Because of the warm, dark tones of his work, Horemans was nicknamed "the dark Horemans." It is not possible to make a clear division between the work of Jan Josef the Elder and his son Jan Josef the Younger, who painted in a similar style. Jan Josef the Elder died in the town of his birth in 1759.

H. Gerson and E. H. ter Kuile   Art and Architecture in Belgium 1600-1800   London, 1960

Reception of the Abbé of St. Michel
(detail)
Antwerp, Mus. Royal des B-A.

HIS WORKS INCLUDE

Shoemaker's Shop, 1712
Vienna, Kunsthist. Mus.
Village School, 1712
Vienna, Kunsthist. Mus.
Musical Company, 1715
Brunswick, Herzog Anton Ulrich-Mus.

See also page 189

Self-portrait, 1895
Amsterdam, Rijksmus.

ISAAC ISRAELS   1865-1934

An impressionistic painter of café and cabaret themes

Isaac Israels was born in Amsterdam in 1865, the son of the painter Joseph Israels. He stayed a very short time at the Hague Academy. Until 1903 he lived in Amsterdam, after which he was active chiefly at The Hague, together with George Hendrik Breitner, Floris Verster, and Suze Robertson. He eventually became one of the most important painters of the generation that succeeded the Hague School.

From 1903 to 1914 Israels studied in Paris, from time to time traveling in Europe. In 1921 he made a trip to Java, where he painted a series of works in which he conveyed the delicate atmosphere of that country and its people. Israels possessed a splendid virtuosity. Because of this and because of his subject-matter, which included representations from the world of cabaret, the circus, the boulevard, and the café, he is often compared with the French painters of his day. His work, however, is essentially different from theirs.

Israels' *Homage to Vincent van Gogh* demonstrates his admiration for this painter, but there is no relationship between the two artists in style. His technical virtuosity betrayed him sometimes into a somewhat superficial art. He also painted portraits, nudes, town views, and pictures of the seashore. He produced some remarkable watercolors, as well as etchings, pastels, and drawings.

ISAAC ISRAELS

HIS WORKS INCLUDE

The Firing Squad, 1881
Utrecht, Cent. Mus. der Gemeente
Javanese Girl
Haarlem, Teyler's Mus.

See also pages 199, 255

The Shop Window
Amsterdam, Rijksmus.

The Trumpet Lesson at the Barracks, 1881
The Hague, Rijksmus. Hendrik Willem Mesdag

JOSEPH ISRAELS 1824-1911

A painter of landscapes and genre scenes

Joseph Israels was born in Groningen in Holland in 1824. At the age of 16 he went to Amsterdam, where he became a pupil of Jan Kruseman. In 1845 he went to Paris and there frequented the studios of Eugène Delacroix, Horace Vernet, and James Pradier. His teacher at this time, however, was François Picot. During his lifetime Israels exhibited many times at the Paris Salon, and in 1878 was made an Officer of the Legion of Honor.

Israels was a painter of portraits, landscapes, seascapes, still-lifes, and historical events. He acquired considerable fame as a watercolorist. His early pictures of genre scenes are in the 17th-century Dutch tradition, but current styles of painting, in particular those of the Romantics and the Impressionists, were a considerable influence on his work. His paintings of seascapes with figures are among his most praiseworthy works, several of them possessing the sentiment generally associated with 19th-century England. He was much occupied, as were the majority of his contemporaries, with the effects of light. Many of his pictures show Dutch peasants silhouetted against windows and cloudy skies. His history paintings are formal and in the Dutch tradition. In many cases they show the clear influence of Rembrandt, both in their lighting and in the method of painting.

Joseph Israels' fame spread during his lifetime to practically every European capital. Van Gogh was strongly influenced by Israels' human approach. His works are to be found in the Rijksmuseum, Amsterdam, in Dordrecht, Groningen, and in several other European cities. Israels died at The Hague in 1911. His son, Isaac Israels, was also a painter.

Woman at the Window
Rotterdam, Boymans-van Beuningen

HIS WORKS INCLUDE

The Shipwrecked, 1861
London, N. G.

The Philosopher, about 1890
London, N. G.

Gossips, 1897
Amsterdam, Rijksmus.

Farm Interior at Laren, 1905
Amsterdam, Rijksmus.

See also page 254

See also page 254

J Israels.

The Happy Family (detail) about 1876
Glasgow, Art Gall.

The Frugal Meal, about 1880
Glasgow, Art Gall.

HIS WORKS INCLUDE

Ruins of the Château de Rosemont
1861
Paris, Louvre
Beach at Sainte-Adresse, 1863
Paris, Mus. de l'Impressionnisme
La Ciotat, 1880
Rotterdam, Boymans-van Beuningen
View of Overschie
Rotterdam, Boymans-van Beuningen

See also pages 198, 239

A Dutch precursor of Impressionism

Johan Barthold Jongkind was an important figure in the development of Impressionism, particularly through his influence on Claude Monet. He was born at Lattrop, near Rotterdam, on June 3, 1819, and studied under the landscape painter Andreas Schelfhout, at the Academy of The Hague. In 1845 he met Eugène Isabey, who influenced his early work. The following year he went to Paris, where he worked under Isabey and François Picot, exhibiting at the Paris Salon in 1848, and again in 1852. Two famous art critics and writers, first Charles Baudelaire and later Émile Zola, admired and wrote of him in several magazines and newspapers.

Jongkind divided his time for some years between The Hague, Paris, and the Normandy coast. At an exhibition arranged by Count Doria, his works were exhibited with paintings by Jean Baptiste Camille Corot, Charles Daubigny, and Constantin Troyon. He underwent great hardship, and also suffered from persecution mania and depressions. In 1860 Corot, Isabey, Théodore Rousseau, and François Bonvin organized a sale for his profit, and in the same year Monet com-

Rotterdam in the Moonlight, 1881
Amsterdam, Rijksmus.

mented on Jongkind's crazed state of mind in a letter to Eugène Boudin. When Jongkind was painting in Le Havre, he had been introduced to Monet, who in turn introduced him to Boudin in 1862. Jongkind was to play an important part in Monet's early development, exercising on him a more decisive influence than that of Boudin. He helped the young Monet to develop his abilities, and to look closely and clearly at nature.

Jongkind's own style had matured by about 1860 and, although he did not paint in oils in the open, he made many vivid sketches and watercolors direct from nature, always trying to show exactly what he saw before him. In 1864 he painted two views of Notre Dame in Paris, one seen on a winter morning, the other at sunset. In this way the real subject of his paintings became the conditions of atmosphere and light of the moment rather than the actual object before him.

In later years Jongkind traveled around France, Belgium, and Switzerland with his friend and pupil Madame Fesser, who succeeded to some extent in calming his nervous state. They visited Lake Geneva and Isère, where Jongkind settled after 1880, though he paid occasional visits to Paris. His late works, including views of Isère, were very bold in color. Jongkind ended his life in a state of madness, dying at Côte-Saint-André, Isère, on February 9, 1891.

The Port
Brussels, Mus. Royaux des B.-A.

JACOB JORDAENS   1593-1678

A Flemish Baroque painter of religious and domestic themes

Jacob Jordaens was born in Antwerp in 1593 and died there in 1678. After the death of Rubens in 1640, he was considered the finest Flemish artist of his time. Like Rubens, Jordaens studied under Adam van Noort while still a boy. He married van Noort's daughter in 1616. Two years later he painted his first picture of which the date is known— *The Adoration of the Kings*, 1618, now in Stockholm. By this time he was already a member of the guild of painters, elected to it on the strength of his watercolors, many of which are still in existence.

For a time Jordaens continued painting religious subjects. They include *The Martyrdom of St. Apollonia*, 1628, in the Augustijnenkerk, Antwerp, and *The Four Evangelists*, about 1625, in the Louvre. These conformed to the painting conventions of his age and were not in the least typical of the natural bent of his mind. He far preferred the Flemish outlook on life, which showed a penchant for depicting jolly, red faces, and fat, well-fed bodies. His painting began to assume an unattractive crudity, with harsh color and violent movement.

When he was about 40, Jordaens came far more directly under the influence of Rubens, and the crudity of his color and draftsmanship gradually gave place to a style of much more pleasing effect. The colors became more gentle, the figures more graceful, the contrasts less forced. In the years about 1640 he painted the *Satyr at the Peasant's House* and *The Triumph of Bacchus*, which are among the works that show him at his best. Later still Jordaens reached a yet higher standard, commanding a notable brilliance and richness of color, as in the *Fruitseller*, about

Portrait of Admiral de Ruyter
Paris, Louvre

HIS WORKS INCLUDE

The Four Evangelists, about 1625
Paris, Louvre

The Martyrdom of St. Apollonia, 1628
Antwerp, Augustijnenkerk

Prometheus, about 1645
Cologne, Wallraf-Richartz-Mus.

Christ among the Doctors, 1663
Mainz, Gemäldegal.

See also pages 158, 227

1650, and *The Triumph of Prince Frederik Hendrik*, 1652. Jordaens was an artist of many talents and at one time had a great number of pupils. His portraits were numerous and highly prized. He also made designs for tapestries and carried out many schemes of mural decoration.

Catalogue of the Jacob Jordaens Exhibition   Mortimer Brand Gall., New York, 1940
H. Gerson and E. H. ter Kuile   Art and Architecture in Belgium 1600-1800   London, 1960

The Hospital Sisters of Antwerp
Antwerp, Mus. Royal des B-A.

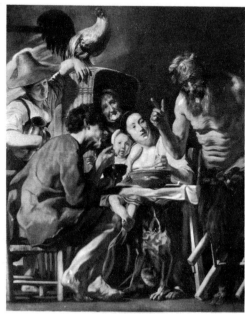

Satyr at the Peasant's House, about 1640
Brussels, Mus. Royaux des B-A.

HIS WORKS INCLUDE

The Cup of the Guild of St. Martin
Haarlem, St. Martin

Relief above the Main Door
Amsterdam, Textile Factory

See also pages 268, 269

HENDRIK DE KEYSER   1565-1621

A celebrated and successful sculptor and architect

Hendrik de Keyser, born in Utrecht in 1565, trained under Cornelis Bloemaert. There is no evidence that he traveled to Italy, as many of his contemporaries did. The strongest influences on his work were those of the classical tradition in Holland. His architectural works formed a link between this tradition and the ornamental style of the Netherlandish Renaissance.

Most of de Keyser's work was executed in Amsterdam. In 1594 he was appointed municipal stonemason and sculptor of Amsterdam, and from 1612 onward was the municipal architect. His Amsterdam Exchange, begun between 1608 and 1613, has since been destroyed, but it must have been very close in design to Sir Thomas Gresham's Exchange in London. The church he built for the city between

1603 and 1614, the South Church, was the first Protestant church to be built in the Netherlands. The design was extremely severe, and there was no altar or choir, so that all attention focused on the pulpit. It employed a combination of Renaissance ideas and Gothic principles. The West Church, which de Keyser started in 1620, was his greatest building. The ground plan follows a pattern similar to that of the South Church, but the decorations are less severe. He also built a number of towers in the city, and in 1606 the East India House.

De Keyser was perhaps the most important Dutch sculptor of his day. He executed numerous terracotta busts, which were modeled with great liveliness and directness. In 's Hertogenbosch he carried out sculptural decorations of insane men and women, executed with great intensity. The most important of de Keyser's sculptural works is the tomb of William the Silent, Prince of Orange, at Delft, commissioned in 1616, in which there are two figures of the prince—one in a life-like attitude and the other as he appeared when dead.

The English sculptor Nicholas Stone became de Keyser's son-in-law, and was also his pupil. When de Keyser died in Amsterdam on May 15, 1621, his sons Pieter, Willem, and Hendrik continued his workshop, but failed to maintain his high standard.

Portrait of Abraham van Goorle: from a medallion, 1599
The Hague, Mauritshuis

Tomb of William the Silent, Prince of Orange, about 1616
Delft, Nieuwe Kerk

The Pharisee and the Publican: from a stained glass window, 1597
Gouda, St. John's

FERNAND KHNOPFF

1858-1921

A Belgian Symbolist painter, draftsman, engraver, and sculptor

Fernand Khnopff was born in Frembergen, Belgium, on September 12, 1858. He became a student of law in Brussels, and at the same time was a pupil of Xavier Mellery, who introduced him to Symbolism. This influence was strengthened when he met Gustave Moreau in Paris in 1879. His work also shows the influence of the English Pre-Raphaelite painters.

Khnopff, an educated man, believed in the interrelation of the arts. His whole creative activity was aimed at achieving this ideal, and he made many illustrations for the contemporary Symbolist poets. Many of his other works have literary subjects. He also produced sensitive landscapes and portraits.

In 1883 Khnopff was one of the founder members of Les XX, an exhibiting society of painters of significance in the development of modern art. Artists who exhibited with Les XX include Georges Seurat, Paul Gauguin, Vincent van Gogh, Auguste Rodin, and James Abbott McNeill Whistler. Khnopff died in Brussels in 1921.

I Lock My Door Upon Myself, 1891
Munich, Neue Pin.

PHILIPS DE KONINCK

A painter of landscapes

Philips de Koninck was born in Amsterdam in 1619, some 12 years later than Rembrandt, whose pupil he was and whose influence can be seen in his work.

Koninck became a highly accomplished landscape painter. His works include some superbly sweeping views of the flat Dutch countryside. These are distinguished by an obvious delight in the contrast of sunlight and shadow and in the splendid dramatic effect of dark, heavy clouds moving over blue skies.

Koninck was one of the very few pupils of Rembrandt to become a landscape painter, but he was also a portraitist who possessed some of his master's skill, as is shown by his *Self-portrait* in the Uffizi Gallery, Florence. He died in 1688 and was buried in Amsterdam.

Landscape, 1655
Firle Place, Sussex, England, Gage Coll.

HIS WORKS INCLUDE

River Landscape, 1664
Rotterdam, Boymans-van Beuningen

Portrait of Joost van den Vondel at the Age of 87, 1674
Amsterdam, Rijksmus.

Landscape, 1676
Amsterdam, Rijksmus.

See also page 186

LUCAS VAN LEYDEN

A brilliant draftsman

Lucas, called "van Leyden," was born Lucas Jacobz, the son of an artist who was his first master. The date of his birth was probably 1494. He astonished his father's friends by his precocity. At the age of nine he was making engravings after his own drawings, and he painted *St. Hubert* when he was 12. His second master was Cornelis Engelbrechtsz. Van Leyden married in 1515. In 1521 he was in Antwerp,

The Sermon (detail) 1530
Amsterdam, Rijksmus.

Self-portrait
Brunswick, Herzog Anton Ulrich-Mus.

HIS WORKS INCLUDE

The Temptation of St Anthony, 1511
Brussels, Mus. Royaux des B-A.

Lot and his Daughters, about 1514
Paris, Louvre

The Madonna and Child with Angels, about 1515
West Berlin, Staatl. Mus.

The Madonna and Child with St. Mary Magdalen and a Donor, 1522
Munich, Alte Pin.

See also pages 215, 216

The Adoration of the Golden Calf
(detail) about 1530
Amsterdam, Rijksmus.

where he met Albrecht Dürer, who painted his portrait. He may have become a member of the painters' guild in 1522. He died in 1533.

Apart from his paintings, which are characterized by their fluid brushwork and their often unusual and startling color, van Leyden made many woodcuts and engravings that show the influence of Dürer. They display his brilliant and sensitive draftsmanship and the inventiveness typical of Northern artists. Traditionally, van Leyden is supposed to have been something of a dandy and *bon vivant*, but the size and quality of his output are not altogether consistent with this legend.

E. G. Troche   Painting in the Netherlands in the 15th and 16th Centuries   London, 1936
M. Davies   The Early Netherlandish School, N. G. Catalogue   London, 1955

Self-portrait of the Artist Aged Forty,
1855   *Brussels, Mus. Royaux des B-A*

HIS WORKS INCLUDE

Flemish Wedding in the 17th Century,
1839
Antwerp, Mus. Royal des B-A.

Restoration of the Roman Catholic
Worship in Antwerp in 1585, 1845
Brussels, Mus. Royaux des B-A.

The Mass of Berthal de Haze, 1854
Brussels, Mus. Royaux des B-A.

Albrecht Dürer Visiting Antwerp in
1520, 1855
Antwerp, Mus. Royal des B-A.

Portrait of the Artist's Daughter, Lucy
1865
Antwerp, Mus. Royal des B-A.

See also page 193

HENDRIK LEYS   1815-1869

A Romantic painter of Belgian history

Hendrik Leys was born in Antwerp, on February 18, 1815. He attended the Antwerp Academy, where he studied under Gustave Wappers, and was also a pupil of his brother-in-law Ferdinand de Braekeleer from 1830 to 1835. Throughout the latter part of his career he was to adhere to an uncompromising archaism, but in the earlier days, after a visit to Paris from which he returned in 1833, he was influenced by the Romantic movement and Eugène Delacroix. It is always possible to detect in his work his latest artistic enthusiasm.

Leys went to Holland and was influenced by Dutch genre painting. He studied Gerard Terborch, Gabriel Metzu, and especially Rembrandt. When he traveled to Germany in 1852, he was impressed by the German primitives. Success came easily and consistently to Leys. He was created a baron in 1862, and was a member both

Scene from the Small Leys Room, about 1855
Antwerp, Town Hall

of the Belgian Royal Academy and the Antwerp Academy. He won medals in Paris at the International Exhibitions of 1862 and 1867.

In 1861 Leys was commissioned to decorate the Salle d'Honneur of Antwerp Town Hall with large mural compositions and portraits of 12 dukes of Brabant. He began in 1863, and was still working on this commission in 1869, the year of his death. After his death, some mural paintings from the dining room of his own house were transferred to the Town Hall. His decorative schemes were sumptuous, representing scenes of family and social life in the 16th century, and in his own time had much influence on decorators in Antwerp. They are among the most important examples of mural painting in the Belgian School of the 19th century. He died on August 26, 1869, and was greatly mourned by the citizens of Antwerp, who erected a statue in his honor soon after his death.

Scene from the Large Leys Room, 1863-69
Antwerp, Town Hall

JAN GOSSAERT called MABUSE   died about 1533

An artist who introduced Italian motifs into Flemish art

Jan Gossaert was born the son of a bookbinder in Maubeuge, Hainault. His master is unknown, but his early style reflects the influences of Hugo van der Goes and Gerard David. It is probable that he had his first training in the Netherlands. In 1503 he registered in the Antwerp guild under the name Jennyn of Hainault. Later he was called Mabuse, which is the Flemish for Maubeuge.

Mabuse was employed first by Jean Carondelet, chancellor of Burgundy, and then by Bastard Philip of Burgundy. When Philip was sent on a mission from Margaret of Austria to Pope Julius II, Mabuse went with him, and made a series of drawings for him of Italian antiquities. Returning to the Netherlands in the following year, he began to incorporate in his own work his knowledge of florid Italian architectural decoration and Italian ideals of beauty. The Italian historian Guicciardini referred to him as "the first Netherlander to bring from Italy the art of painting history and poesy with nude figures." His subjects include such classical figures as Venus and Cupid, Neptune and Amphitrite, previously unknown in Flemish art. His plump, muscular nudes do not conform to the Flemish fashion of narrow shoulders, small breasts, and large hips, but resemble more nearly Italian models. His work is spoiled by an abundance of detail, and by his lack of any real understanding of Renaissance art.

Portrait of Jean Carondelet
Paris, Louvre

In 1516 Mabuse designed a carriage for the memorial ceremonies for Ferdinand of Aragon, and there are records of payment for two portraits of Eleanora, sister of Charles V of Spain. The next year Philip was made Bishop of Utrecht, and Mabuse accompanied him on his journey there. At this time Jan van Scorel was his pupil.

When Philip died, Mabuse was patronized by his nephew, Adolphe of Burgundy.

He designed a memorial to Isabella of Burgundy, the queen of the refugee king, Christian II of Denmark, who had been Adolphe's guest in 1523. King Henry VIII of England owned a painting by Mabuse. In 1527 Mabuse went on tour with Lucas van Leyden to Antwerp and Malines, where he was to work in his last years at the court of Margaret of Austria, regent of the Netherlands. He died about 1533.

J. G. van Gelder   Jan Gossaert in Rome, 1508-1509   Amsterdam, 1942
H. B. Wehle and M. Salinger   Early Flemish, Dutch, and German Painters, Met. Mus. Catalogue
    Cambridge, Mass., 1947

The Madonna and Child
Paris, Louvre

The Adoration of the Magi (detail) about 1508
London, N. G.

NICOLAS MAES   1634-1693

A pupil of Rembrandt who painted domestic scenes

Nicolas Maes was born in Dordrecht in 1634. He entered the studio of Rembrandt in 1650, and was his pupil for about four years. He returned to Dordrecht in 1654 and, while still a young man, painted a number of pictures in the style of Rembrandt, with lifesize figures and with much of the rich, glowing color that he must have admired in his master.

From 1655 Maes lived in Antwerp, and after 1673 resided in Amsterdam until his death in 1693. In his middle years he liked to paint scenes of the life around him: old women at the spinning-wheel, girls looking out of windows, the preparation of a meal, or the reading of the Bible. *The Idle Servant* is a typical example of his work of this period.

Later in life, Maes gave up the genre picture for the portrait. He abandoned the

76

influence of Rembrandt and adopted the easy, elegant sophistication of Anthony van Dyck. His portraits were still of considerable distinction. It is, however, for his earlier works, particularly the many depictions of card players, that Maes is most famous.

N. Maclaren *The Dutch School, N. G. Catalogue* London, 1960

The Lovers
London, Apsley House

The Idle Servant, 1655
London, N. G.

Portrait of a Young Man, about 1675
Amsterdam, Rijksmus.

JAKOB MARIS	1837-1899
MATTHIJS MARIS	1839-1917
WILLEM MARIS	1844-1910

Three brothers who continued Dutch traditions in the 19th century

The three Maris brothers were born at The Hague: Jakob in 1837, Matthijs in 1839, and Willem in 1844. Jakob was a student in Antwerp and then in Paris where he remained from 1865 until 1871. There he was influenced by Jean Baptiste Camille Corot and Henri Fantin-Latour. He began by painting minutely detailed scenes of Dutch domestic life, depicting its most typical aspects. He also painted bridges, mills, quays, and canals with an impressionistic technique. He was particularly skilled in rendering the effects of sun shining through mist.

JAKOB MARIS
Fishing Boat at Scheveningen
Amsterdam, Rijksmus.

Matthijs studied at the academies of The Hague and Antwerp until 1858. Except for a journey along the Rhine, he worked with his brother Jakob at The Hague and in Paris, where he remained until 1875. Two years later he went to London and worked for Daniel Cottier, an English art dealer. At first he painted in a realistic style, producing landscapes and portraits. Later his style became visionary and emotive. He was inspired by the German Romantic school and the English Pre-Raphaelites.

The third and youngest brother, Willem, painted in a different and less sensitive

M Maris.

WILLEM MARIS

Ducks Alighting on a Pool
London, N. G.

Cows near a Ditch
Amsterdam, Rijksmus.

Willem Maris

style. He portrayed cattle in the sun, sand-dunes, and fields with light accentuating their colors. His work is somewhat uniform.

Jakob Maris died in 1899. Willem died 11 years later in the city of his birth, and Matthijs in London in 1917.

D. C. Thomson   *The Brothers Maris*   Rand, Australia, 1907
E. D. Friedländer   *Matthew Maris*   London, 1921
N. Maclaren   *The Dutch School, N. G. Catalogue*   London, 1960

MATTHIJS MARIS
Fairy Tale (detail)
Amsterdam, Rijksmus.

WILLEM MARIS
Meadow with Cows
Amsterdam, Rijksmus.

Erasmus of Rotterdam, 1517
Rome, Gall. Corsini

QUENTIN MASSYS   1464/5-1530

An artist who amalgamated the traditions of Flemish art with classical Renaissance motifs

Quentin Massys was an important artist of the Antwerp School, a highly versatile painter of religious subjects, portraits, and everyday scenes. Born in Louvain in 1464/5, he was first apprenticed to his father, a blacksmith and clockmaker, but later took up painting. In 1491 he moved to Antwerp, prior to which he was possibly in the workshop of Albrecht, the son of Dieric Bouts. Two years later he joined the Antwerp guild as a master painter.

At that time Antwerp was the center in the Netherlands of commerce, learning, and the arts, and Massys was duly caught up in the city's prosperity. His house became a meeting-place for humanist scholars, most notably Erasmus and Peter Gillies, whose portraits he painted for their friend Sir Thomas More. More, who later befriended Massys, praised him as the "re-creator of ancient art," a remark in keeping with the classical aspirations of the Renaissance. It was appropriate to Massys' successful amalgamation of these aspirations, which he adopted in Antwerp or on a supposed visit to Italy between 1514 and 1519, with the traditions he inherited from Flemish primitives such as Roger van der Weyden. New Italian features in Massys' paintings were the exotic and sometimes crowding architectural ornament, the realistically relaxed movement of his figures, and the symmetry of their grouping. His characterizations, particularly in his subtly satirical pictures of ordinary life such as *The Moneylender and his Wife*, 1514, are full of insight into the intricacies of facial expression. They are probably the result of a study of Leonardo's caricatures, which were to prompt such Flemish subjects as Marinus van Roejmerswaelen's contorted *Tax Gatherers*, and culminate in the tavern scenes of 100 years later.

In 1520 Dürer came to visit Massys and saw the splendid frescoed house he had just built, but missed Massys himself, who was away. The elder Hans Holbein also came to see him, and Joachim Patenier was a friend. Patenier painted landscape backgrounds to some of Massys' pictures, and Massys became the guardian of Patenier's children when they were orphaned in 1524. Massys married twice and had 12 children, two of whom, Jan and Cornelis, were painters and were much influenced by their father's work. He died in 1530.

E. G. Troche Painting in the Netherlands in the 15th and 16th Centuries   London, 1936

HIS WORKS INCLUDE

Altarpiece of the St. Anne Brotherhood in Louvain, 1509
Brussels, Mus. Royaux des B-A.

The Entombment, about 1511
Antwerp, Mus. Royal des B-A.

The Madonna and Child Enthroned, about 1520
West Berlin, Staatl. Mus.

See also page 142

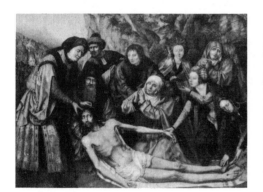

The Entombment (detail) about 1511
Antwerp, Mus. Royal des B-A.

The Madonna and Child with St. Barbara and St. Catherine, late work   *London, N. G.*

St. Mary Magdalen, about 1525
Antwerp, Mus. Royal des B-A.

MASTER OF FLÉMALLE
sometimes identified
with ROBERT CAMPIN   1378/9-1444

A painter whose style was revolutionary in its naturalism

The most satisfactory identification of the anonymous master who was wrongly supposed to have come from Flémalle is that he is Robert Campin. Campin was a painter of Tournai, born in 1378 or 1379, and his name appears in the records of that town from about 1405 until his death in 1444. In 1406 and 1444 he received payment for work done for the town council. In 1423 he took part in a strike against

See also page 127

the nobility, but was elected dean of the Guild of St. Luke in the same year. In 1432 he was sentenced to one year's banishment for openly living with his mistress, Leurence Pollette. This sentence was, however, commuted to a fine on the intervention of the Countess of Hainault.

No pictures are certainly known to be Campin's, but he had two famous pupils, Jacques Daret and Roger van der Weyden. It is these pupils that connect his name with that of the so-called Master of Flémalle. The works attributed to that artist are revolutionary in their naturalism. His treatment of religious themes is intimate and realistic, with delightful details of everyday life. A Madonna who warms her hands by the fire is a typical example. Such characteristics established the Flemish School as distinct from the French School. The same realism is apparent in the portraits attributed to Campin in which a brilliant draftsmanship is shown.

Portrait of a Man, early work
London, N. G.

The Madonna and Child
before a Fire Screen
(detail) before 1430
London, N. G.

The Annunciation with Donors and St. Joseph: from the
Mérode Altarpiece, 1425-28
New York, Met. Mus., Cloisters Coll., Purchase

MASTER OF JOACHIM AND ANNA   active 15th century

An anonymous sculptor of insight and feeling

The Master of Joachim and Anna was an anonymous sculptor active in Utrecht or Haarlem in the 15th century. His name has been derived from a piece representing the meeting of Joachim and Anna, now in the Rijksmuseum, Amsterdam. He was a contemporary of the Utrecht sculptor Adriaen van Wesel.

The Master of Joachim and Anna combined in his work an observation of reality with a feeling of spirituality. On stylistic grounds there are two more statues attributed to him — *The Birth of Our Lady*, now in Berlin, and a *Madonna* in a private collection in The Hague. His work has some affinities with that of Dieric Bouts and Geertgen tot Sint Jans.

See also page 262

ANTON MAUVE

A landscape painter of the Hague School

Anton Mauve was born in Zaandam in the Netherlands in 1838, and from an early age had a strong desire to become a painter, in spite of opposition from his family. He became a pupil of Pieter Frederik van Os, and later of Walter Verschuur. From 1856 until 1859 Mauve was painting with Willem Maris and Johannes Warnadus Bilders in Oosterbeek. In 1865 he moved to Amsterdam for some time, and by 1870 he was in Haarlem. During the following years Mauve lived at The Hague and in Laren, the Dutch "Barbizon." He gave drawing lessons to his cousin Vincent van Gogh when the latter came to The Hague late in 1882. Mauve always suffered from poor health and he was subject to fits of depression. He died in Arnhem in 1888.

Mauve's work was much appreciated, particularly in England and the United States. He won medals for his painting in Vienna, Philadelphia, Antwerp, and, in 1888, in Paris. Mauve always painted in a low key, and his paintings show his remarkable ability to render the effects of light, both in oil and watercolor. He produced some portraits and marine scenes, but most of his works were scenes of wild heath or marshland with pasturing animals. With Joseph Israels and Jakob Maris, Mauve was a leader of the Hague School.

Morning Ride along the Beach
Amsterdam, Rijksmus.

HIS WORKS INCLUDE

Studio of the Painter
Pieter Frederik van Os, 1856
Amsterdam, Rijksmus.
Kitchen Garden
Amsterdam, Rijksmus.
Snow at Scheveningen
Amsterdam, Rijksmus.

See also page 243

Marshlands
Amsterdam, Rijksmus.

HANS MEMLING

A painter of portraits and religious subjects

Hans Memling was born about 1433 in Seligenstadt near Frankfurt. Tradition has it that he first came to Bruges as a wounded soldier and was nursed back to health by the brothers of the Hospital of St. John. He later painted a picture for them in return for this service. He probably served his apprenticeship in Cologne, and, from 1467, he worked under Roger van der Weyden. He became a prosperous citizen of Bruges, and owned two houses there.

In 1468 Memling collaborated with Bouts and Hugo van der Goes on the decorations for the wedding of Charles the Bold and Margaret of York. One of the courtiers who attended the bride was Sir John Donne of Kidwelly, who commissioned Memling to paint the triptych now in the National Gallery, London. This is his earliest known painting.

Memling's work, which consists of both religious subjects and portraits, closely followed the style of his master. In fact, he collaborated with van der Weyden on several altarpieces. His portraits were in great demand. Owing to the thriving trade between the port of Bruges and Italy, he was known and admired in Florence

The Madonna and Child
West Berlin, Staatl. Mus.

HIS WORKS INCLUDE

The Passion, about 1470
Turin, Gall. Sabauda

The Seven Joys of the Virgin,
about 1480
Munich, Alte Pin.

The Madonna Enthroned between
Two Angels, about 1480
Florence, Uffizi

Triptych of the Mystic Marriage
of St. Catherine
Bruges, Hospital of St. John

Triptych of the Resurrection
Paris, Louvre

See also pages 136, 137

and received many commissions from this city. The considerable amount of property Memling left when he died in 1494 is an indication of his success as a painter. His clean draftsmanship and strong, pure areas of color, decoratively used, were characteristic of the Flemish primitives. After Memling the art of the Netherlands turned toward Italian ideals of beauty and Italian concepts of spatial composition and chiaroscuro.

H. H. J. Weale   Hans Memling   London, 1865
E. G. Troche   Painting in the Netherlands in the 15th and 16th Centuries   London, 1936
M. Guillaume-Linephty   Hans Memling in the Hospital of St. John at Bruges   Paris, 1939

The Madonna and Child
West Berlin, Staatl. Mus.

The Madonna and Child with Saints, Angels and Donors: from the Donne Triptych, about 1468
London, N. G.

The Return of the Miners (detail)
about 1895
Ixelles, Brussels, Mus. Constantin Meunier

CONSTANTIN MEUNIER   1831-1905

A painter and sculptor concerned with a new social realism

Constantin Meunier was born on April 12, 1831, in Etterbeek, a suburb of Brussels. He first came into contact with artists in his mother's boarding house, and later he attended the Brussels Academy, where he studied sculpture under Charles Auguste Fraikin. He was, however, also attracted to painting and went to the atelier run by the painter François Joseph Navez. At this stage Meunier's style was insipid and academic.

Meunier first exhibited at the Brussels Salon in 1851. About three years later he abandoned sculpture and turned to painting, possibly on the advice of Charles de Groux, with whom he became friendly. Together they frequented the Saint-Luc Studio, and Meunier was certainly influenced by his friend. He made designs for stained glass and fabrics, and produced many religious paintings. These clearly reveal the influence of Jean François Millet and Gustave Courbet. Meunier frequently stayed in the Westmalle Trappist monastery, where he made studies for many pictures, including *The Burial of a Trappist Monk*, 1860.

In 1862 Meunier married, and settled down to a happy domestic life. He turned to historical painting and produced a series, *Episodes of the Peasants' War*. The turning point of his career was his discovery, in 1878, of the industrial world and its pictorial possibilities. Four years later his work was interrupted by a government mission to Spain, but he returned in 1883 to Brussels. He was appointed professor at the Louvain Academy. In 1885 he again took up sculpture, in which he carried on the industrial subject-matter of his later paintings. His vast *Monument to Labor*, which was acquired by the Belgian government, remained unfinished. In 1893 he collaborated with the sculptor Karel van der Stappen on a scheme of decorations for the Brussels Botanical Gardens and with the Frenchman Félix Maurice Charpentier on a monument to Émile Zola. Meunier exhibited in Paris on several occasions. His social realism, part of a widespread movement on the European continent in reaction to 19th-century academic art, has been particularly influential in East European countries. His approach offers a parallel to the early works of Vincent van Gogh. His technique was an innovation in the history of Belgian sculpture. He represented scenes of the life of the miners, and the misery of the working people from the industrial areas of Belgium. Constantin Meunier died in Brussels in 1905.

HIS WORKS INCLUDE

The Ironworker, 1886
Brussels, Mus. Royaux des B-A.
Tobacco Factory at Seville, 1889
Brussels, Mus. Royaux des B-A.
The Sower: from the Monument
to Labor, 1898
Brussels, Parc du Cinquantenaire
Industry: from the Monument
to Labor, 1898
Brussels, Parc du Cinquantenaire
Coal Depot in Snow
Brussels, Mus. Royaux des B-A.

See also pages 247, 278, 279

The Martyrdom of St. Stephen
(detail) 1867
Antwerp, Mus. Royal des B-A.

The Harvest: study for relief on the
Monument to Labor, 1898
Antwerp, Mus. Royal des B-A.

CONRAD MEYT   about 1480-1551

A sculptor who was influenced by the Renaissance but who remained essentially Gothic

Conrad Meyt, also known as Conrad van Mechelen, was a German-Swiss, born about 1480. He became master sculptor in the household of Margaret of Austria, Duchess of Savoy, in 1512, for which he received payment of five sous a day. For the ducal art collection, Meyt made marble portrait statues of the duke and duchess and also many little alabaster and bronze figures. Meyt married in the Netherlands in 1514, and in 1536 he was entered as Master Conrad the Sculptor in the roll of the Antwerp guild.

In 1526 Meyt began work on tombs in the Church of St. Nicholas of Tolentin in

HIS WORKS INCLUDE

Judith, about 1514
Munich
Tomb of Margaret of Austria, 1531
Brou, France, St. Nicolas
Strength
Paris, Louvre

See also page 263

Adam and Eve
Vienna, Kunsthist. Mus.

Brou, commissioned by Margaret of Austria in memory of her husband, Philibert of Savoy, who had been killed in a hunting accident. The tomb of Margaret of Austria herself was commissioned from Meyt, and in this church there was also the tomb of Philibert's mother, Margaret of Bourbon. The sculpture and decorations were executed by a team of Flemish sculptors under the direction of Loys van Boghem as master mason. The effigies of the duke and duchess were made by Conrad Meyt and his brother Thomas. After the death of Margaret of Austria, Meyt was given a monetary gift by Emperor Charles V.

Between 1538 and 1549 Conrad Meyt executed statues for the tabernacle of the abbey church of Tongerloo. In his work there are clear influences of Albrecht Dürer and Lucas van Leyden. Although Meyt took over the outer forms of the Renaissance, he remained essentially a Gothic artist. He was mentioned several times by Dürer in his diary of his journey in the Netherlands, and some of Meyt's figures were copied by the young Rubens. Conrad Meyt died in Antwerp in 1551.

HIS WORKS INCLUDE

St. John the Baptist, 1895
Ghent, Mus. des B-A.
Solidarity, 1898
Brussels, Mus. Royaux des B-A.
Fountain with Five Nude Boys
Essen, Folkwang Mus.

See also pages 251, 281, 282, 283

Kneeling Boy, 1925
Mannheim, Kunsthalle

GEORGES MINNE   1866-1941

A sculptor concerned with the expression of religious feeling

Georges Minne was born in Ghent, Belgium, in 1866. He was a pupil of Jean Delvin and studied at the Ghent Academy. He worked in Paris for a short while, and passed the years of World War I in Wales. The major part of his life, however, was spent in the small village of Laethem-Sint-Marten in Belgium.

Minne's chief concern was with the physical expression of suffering, his profound interest in Gothic sculpture being apparent in his elongated treatment of the body. Toward the end of his life his figures became more robust, showing the influence of Auguste Rodin.

Especially famous are Minne's groups of mothers and their children, a theme that recurs frequently in his work in both religious and informal groupings. He also did a number of portrait busts, some of which are characterized by a smile. His portrayals of young people kneeling are among the most distinguished of his works, religious groups also being eminent. Examples of Minne's statues are to be found in Rotterdam, Essen, Mannheim, and several private collections. He died in 1941.

84

JOOS DE MOMPER 1564-1635

An accomplished landscape painter

Landscape with River
Amsterdam, Rijksmus.

Joos de Momper was born in 1564, the son, and later the pupil, of the painter and art dealer, Bartolomeus de Momper. He became a celebrated landscape painter, and was received as a master in the Antwerp painters' guild in 1581. His father was dean of the guild, and in 1611 Joos himself became dean. There is little documentary information about Joos de Momper's life. It is recorded, however, that he was the pupil of "Lodewijk of Trevi," who came from Malines, but that he left his teacher in about 1580.

There are no dated paintings by de Momper, and his style shows no change or development. For some years he worked in collaboration with Pieter Bruegel the Younger, and he was greatly influenced by the latter's style, although he never copied his work. He was a painter of great sensitivity, and in his hands the Mannerist conventions were transformed and given new life. Although de Momper used the conventional elements of fantasy and soft, spacious distances, his technique was spontaneous and the details of his paintings were based on reality. Jan Bruegel the Elder and his son, Jan the Younger, painted small figures into some of de Momper's landscape settings.

It is probable that Joos de Momper had a prosperous studio. He collaborated not only with the Bruegel family, but also with Nicholas van Cleve on a painting, *The Tower of Babel*. De Momper also painted landscape decorations in Rosenborg Castle, Copenhagen, and in Frederiksborg Castle, Hillerød. Some of his paintings were based on landscapes by Hercules Seghers. There is no evidence to prove that de Momper visited Italy and there are few Italian motifs in his work, yet his treatment of mountain themes suggests a journey across the Alps. Joos de Momper died in Antwerp in 1635.

J. Lassaigne   Flemish Painting   New York, 1957/58
H. Gerson and E. H. ter Kuile   Art and Architecture in Belgium 1600-1800   London, 1960

HIS WORKS INCLUDE

Winter Landscape
Cambridge, England, Fitzwm.
Landscape with the Fall of Icarus
Paris, Louvre
The Alps
Kassel, Germany, Hessisches Landesmus.
Mountain Landscape
Vienna, Kunsthist. Mus.

See also page 221

The Flight into Egypt
Oxford, Ashmolean

View of the Scheldt before Antwerp
Munich, Alte Pin.

JAN MONET   about 1484-1550

A sculptor who greatly contributed to the Renaissance in the Netherlands

Jan Monet was born about 1484. His works reflect the decorative style of sculpture of the second half of the 15th century in Italy. It is certain that he traveled at least as far south as the south of France, where he stayed in Aix-en-Provence in 1512. Four years later he was in Spain working with Bartolomé Ordonez in Barcelona.

Returning to Antwerp in 1521, Monet met Albrecht Dürer, and was invested as artist to Emperor Charles V. About three years later, Monet settled in Malines, where he established his permanent workshop. Only one work from his hand is known that possesses both his signature and a date: an alabaster retable of 1533 in a Roman Catholic church in Halle. Many other retables and monuments are also attributed to him. With Conrad Meyt, Jan Monet contributed much to the early Renaissance in the Netherlands. He died in 1550.

Self-portrait, 1558
Florence, Uffizi

SIR ANTHONIS MOR   about 1521-1576/77

A court portrait painter of the 16th century

Anthonis Mor, born about 1521, was a portrait painter from Utrecht. He studied there in the workshop of the Dutch Romanist, Jan van Scorel. Like van Scorel, Mor traveled to Italy to see the work of Raphael and Michelangelo, and while he was there he became much influenced by Titian.

In 1547 Mor moved to the southern Netherlands, where he is known to have joined the Antwerp painters' guild in the same year. Two years later he was working for Cardinal Granvella, who introduced him to the Spanish court. Mor's aristocratic birth lent him favor at court, and he was made official painter to the Spanish regent, Mary of Hungary. In 1550 Mor was in Italy, and in 1552 he was sent to Spain to paint Mary of Hungary's nephew Philip, later Philip II of Spain, and her sister, Queen Catherine of Portugal. The portrait of Philip was a success. It was included among the personal belongings of Philip's father, Charles V, when he retired to a monastery. Mor also secured another commission, this time to go to England in 1553 and paint Philip's future bride, Mary Tudor. This painting is now in the Prado, Madrid. Mor painted many portraits in England and was knighted by Queen Mary, but he had little influence on the court style already established by Hans Holbein the Younger.

When Philip succeeded to the sovereignty of the Spanish Netherlands, Mor became his court painter in Brussels. The painter was such a favorite of the king that he accompanied Philip back to Spain when he was obliged to withdraw from the Netherlands. However, Mor soon fled to the Netherlands without the king's knowledge and refused to return despite Philip's repeated offers. He wished to stay with his wife, who was in danger of persecution by the Spanish Inquisition, and, indeed, Mor himself also came under suspicion.

In the Netherlands Mor worked in the service of the Duke of Alva, for whom he painted portraits of his several mistresses. He settled in Antwerp and remained there until his death in 1576/77. He had many children, one of whom had accompanied him to Spain but had disappeared in Africa during the campaign of King Sebastian of Portugal.

Anthonis Mor established an international tradition in portrait painting which was to influence the work of van Dyck and Velázquez.

J. Denucé Inventories of the Art Collection in Antwerp in the 16th and 17th Centuries Antwerp, 1932

HIS WORKS INCLUDE

The Duke of Alva, 1549
New York, Hispanic Soc.
Empress Maria of Austria, 1551
Madrid, Prado
Portrait of Jan van Scorel, 1560
London, Society of Antiquaries
Sir Henry Lee, 1568
London, N. P. G.
Gentleman with a Dog, 1569
Washington, D. C., N. G.

See also page 152

The Buffoon Pejeron
Madrid, Prado

Mary Tudor, Queen of England, 1554
Madrid, Prado

FRANÇOIS JOSEPH NAVEZ

1787-1869

The founder of the realistic school in Belgium

François Joseph Navez was born in 1787. In Paris he was a pupil of Jacques Louis David and was greatly influenced by him. Navez remained a classicist his whole life, painting chiefly religious compositions, portraits, and historical subjects. In 1833 he was made director of the Brussels Academy, and attracted many pupils to his studio. His portraits are objective and have a satiny texture that is very similar to David's work. Navez died in Brussels in 1869.

L. van Puyvelde   F. J. Navez   Brussels, 1931

HIS WORKS INCLUDE

Portrait of the Painter
Jacques Louis David, 1817
Brussels, Mus. Royaux des B-A.

The Meeting of Isaac and Rebecca
1826
Amsterdam, Rijksmus.

Athaliah and Joash, 1830
Brussels, Mus. Royaux des B-A.

The Holy Family, 1848
Antwerp, Mus. Royal des B-A.

The Judgment of Solomon, 1855
Antwerp, Mus. Royal des B-A.

See also page 192

The Holy Family (detail) 1848
Antwerp, Mus. Royal des B-A.

AERT VAN DER NEER

1603/4-1677

A painter of moonlit landscapes

Until 1630 Aert van der Neer, born in Amsterdam in 1603 or 1604, lived in Gorichem, where he was bailiff of the van Arkel family. In 1630 he moved with his wife, Lysbeth Goverts, back to Amsterdam, where he devoted himself to painting, though he kept a wineshop from 1658 to 1662. He died in 1677.

Van der Neer's first dated work is of 1635 and shows the influence of Joachim Camphuysen and Raphael. He painted canal views, winter landscapes, and nocturnal fireside scenes, but his most typical works are moonlit landscapes. These have a poetic atmosphere stressed in the rendering of light, which is reflected from water, land, and cloudy sky. His winter landscapes, enlivened with small figures rather in the manner of Hendrick Avercamp, are in pale blues, silvery-grays, and pinks, colors that were to be echoed in 19th-century Dutch romantic landscapes. Van der Neer painted many delightful works, although their quality varied.

N. Maclaren   The Dutch School, N. G. Catalogue   London, 1960

HIS WORKS INCLUDE

River Scene by Moonlight, about 1645
Amsterdam, Rijksmus.

Scene on a Canal
London, Wallace Coll.

Landscape at Sunrise
The Hague, Mauritshuis

Frost Scene
Amsterdam, Rijksmus.

See also page 185

ADRIAEN VAN OSTADE

1610-1685

A painter of peasant life

Adriaen van Ostade was born in Haarlem in 1610, and died there in 1685. He was the son of a weaver, one of a large family, and his youngest brother, Isaac, also became a notable painter. Adriaen was a pupil of Frans Hals, at the same time as Adriaen Brouwer. These two artists became the typical exponents of those scenes of Dutch low life which interested and attracted so many of their contemporaries.

Van Ostade's peasants are certainly a miserable, stunted, ill-washed assortment of creatures. They convey the impression that this was their normal appearance, that they accepted a dull, dirty, wretched life without protest or hope of better things. This is not altogether surprising, as van Ostade was painting in a country devasted by 70 years of war and reduced to a wretched standard of living.

Pictures with a more urbane and civilized air were also within van Ostade's capabilities. An example is his *Family Group*, in the Louvre, where the father of the family is sitting in a handsomely furnished room, his wife, sons, and five daughters in a line, and a young married couple behind, all looking prosperous and immensely respectable. He also painted religious pictures of beauty and refinement, and was responsible for figures in some of the paintings of Pieter Saenredam and Salomon van Ruysdael. Like many of his contemporaries, van Ostade was an exceedingly industrious painter, leaving about 1000 works. There are also a number of etchings and rather florid watercolors, a branch of painting of which he was an early exponent.

Perhaps the most surprising thing about van Ostade is that any pupil of Frans Hals could have been so free from the influence of his master's geniality and bravura. Evidently he saw life very differently, and was at one with Adriaen Brouwer, Jan Steen, David Teniers the Younger, and others in finding the peasants, their habits and their pastimes, more interesting than the respectable and the worthy.

N. Maclaren The Dutch School, N. G. Catalogue London, 1960

The Alchemist (detail) 1661
London, N. G.

HIS WORKS INCLUDE

Barrel Organ Player by a Cottage
1640
Copenhagen, Statens Mus.
Peasant Courting an Elderly Woman
1652
London, N. G.
Interior of an Inn with a
Hurdy Gurdy Player, 1653
London, N. G.
The Physician in his Study, 1665
West Berlin, Staatl. Mus.
Travelers Resting, 1671
Amsterdam, Rijksmus.

See also pages 175, 234

Interior with Peasants, 1663
London, Wallace Coll.

Interior (detail) 1653
London, N. G.

The Fishmonger, 1673
Amsterdam, Rijksmus.

The Young Bull, 1647
The Hague, Mauritshuis

HIS WORKS INCLUDE

Cattle and Sheep in a
Stormy Landscape, 1647
London, N. G.

Landscape with Cows, Sheep,
and Horses, 1651
London, N. G.

Orpheus Charming the Animals, 1651
Amsterdam, Rijksmus.

Landscape with Cattle, 1653
Amsterdam, Rijksmus.

See also page 236

Cow Looking at itself in the Water
1648
The Hague, Mauritshuis

PAULUS POTTER
1625-1654

A renowned painter of animals

Paulus Potter was born at Enkhuizen, in North Holland, in 1625 and was taught by his father, Pieter Potter, who painted landscapes and figures with distinction. When he was 21 Paulus Potter went to Delft, where he was elected a member of the Guild of St. Luke. A year earlier he had made The Hague his home, and there won the attention of Maurice, Prince of Orange, for whom he painted some of his most famous pictures.

In his early days Potter painted several Biblical pictures, such as *Abraham Entering into Canaan*, now in Nuremberg. Even in this early work it is clear that the subject was chosen as an excuse for portraying Abraham's herds rather than Abraham himself. He next painted *The Young Bull*, 1647, now in the Mauritshuis at The Hague, which has been cited as one of the three most celebrated paintings in Holland. It is extraordinary if only for its dimensions, for it is lifesize, while most contemporary Dutch artists were painting on a small scale. Several of Potter's pictures are lifesize, including *The Bear Hunt* and the equestrian portrait of *Dr. Tulp*, burgomaster of Amsterdam, who persuaded Potter to live in Amsterdam in 1652. *The Young Bull* shows little idea of composition. There is no play of light and shade. None of the subsidiary figures—a cow, a ewe, a ram, and a bearded shepherd—is of importance.

Potter left over 100 pictures, painted in the ten years before he died in 1654 of consumption in Amsterdam. The smaller works, such as the *Cow Looking at itself in the Water*, are considered finer than the large paintings. They are notable for their charming landscape backgrounds, their clear, delicate coloring, and their firmness of execution. Among all the Dutch painters of his time, Paulus Potter stands out for the accuracy, simplicity, and single-mindedness with which he painted what he saw. His paintings of sheep, cattle, and horses are as perfect portraits as those of a Dutch burgher or peasant or housewife by any other artist of the time.

JOHAN THORN PRIKKER
1868-1932

A Symbolist and Art Nouveau painter

Johan Thorn Prikker was born at The Hague on June 5, 1868, and he had to struggle for many years against poverty and lack of recognition. He studied at the Academy of The Hague, and was influenced by George Hendrik Breitner, whose work had in it elements of Impressionism; like Jan Toorop, however, Prikker adopted a divisionist technique. His style then developed away from the Impressionist manner, and he showed his preference for the new aesthetic ideal that was emerging at the end of the 19th century. He became concerned with symbolic representation, rather than the outward appearance of things. He produced, around 1892, a series of drawings of the Life and Passion of Christ. Like James Ensor, he used this subject-matter to express his own sense of persecution.

In 1893 Prikker was invited to exhibit with Les XX in Brussels; he met the Belgian Symbolist writer, Émile Verhaeren, and the painter and architect, Henri van de Velde, a leader of the Art Nouveau movement. In his designs for chairs, chair-covers, carpets, and marquetry, Prikker's style resembled that of van de Velde. He participated in the current enthusiasm for batik-printing, and attained a new beauty in this art in his work for the firm of Utterwijk at The Hague.

After 1893 the use of distortion and of decoration became the outstanding features of Prikker's style. He admired Japanese prints, and shared the growing interest in Oriental art in general. This is apparent in his designs for the third issue of the Belgian magazine "Van Nu en Straks," in 1893. In 1900 he began two years' work on murals for the house of Dr. Leuring, built in The Hague by van de Velde, all in the Art Nouveau style. Prikker settled in Germany in 1904, and died there on March 5, 1932.

ARTUS QUELLINUS the ELDER   1609-1668

A sculptor and decorator who was the master of Flemish Baroque

Artus Quellinus the Elder was born in Antwerp in 1609, the son of the sculptor Erasmus Quellinus. He was related to the painters Artus and Lucas van Uhden. He was trained by his father, and by 1631 he was already working in Rijssel. By 1634 he was engaged in work on the castle of Prince Frederik Hendrik at Hanse-laarsdijk. Quellinus later went to Rome, where he worked in the studio of Frans Duquesnoy. Late in 1639 he returned to Antwerp, and in this year he produced a coat of arms for the Plantin House. He was also a member of the sculptors' guild in Antwerp.

In 1644 Quellinus carved a group, *The Madonna between St. Joseph and St. Anne*,

Justice: detail from the Decapitation of the Sons of Brutus, 1650-64
Amsterdam, Rijksmus.

Model for the Back Façade of Amsterdam Town Hall (detail) 1650-64
Amsterdam, Rijksmus.

Charity
London, V. and A.

in a Baroque, Rubenesque style, for the Church of St. Paul, Antwerp, and soon afterwards he carved *The Madonna Araceli* for the choir of Brussels Cathedral. He went abroad, probably to France, about April, 1644, and the following year was in Lyons with the painter Laureys Francke. There is, however, no proof that he worked on decorations at Fontainebleau as he is sometimes reputed to have done.

Quellinus owned a house in Antwerp in 1645, and he visited Amsterdam in 1646 and 1647. He is reported to have been in Sweden between that year and 1650. In 1650 he was given a very important commission, that of the decorations of the Town Hall in Amsterdam. The work was a tremendous undertaking, and Quellinus stayed in Amsterdam from 1650 until 1664. He was forced to employ numerous assistants, including his cousin Artus Quellinus II, Rombout Verhulst, and the son of the sculptor and architect Hendrik de Keyser. The quality of the work carried out by Quellinus varied, but among the loveliest figures are the caryatids in the Hall of Justice, where the nude bodies were treated in a Rubenesque manner.

While working on these decorations Quellinus also executed other commissions. He carved *Apollo with Nine Muses* for the queen of Sweden, and he produced various monuments and sculptural portraits in Germany and the Netherlands. He owned various properties in Antwerp and in the neighborhood of Amsterdam. Artus Quellinus died in Antwerp in 1668.

Justice, about 1652: study for Hall of Justice, Amsterdam Town Hall
Amsterdam, Rijksmus.

Caryatid, about 1652: study for Hall of Justice, Amsterdam Town Hall
Amsterdam, Rijksmus.

Caryatid, about 1652: study for Hall of Justice, Amsterdam Town Hall
Amsterdam, Rijksmus.

Providence, about 1652: study for Hall of Justice, Amsterdam Town Hall
Amsterdam, Rijksmus.

REMBRANDT VAN RYN
1606-1669

A great artist of immense humanity

Rembrandt was born in 1606, the fifth of six children of a prosperous miller in Leiden, Holland. He adopted the surname van Ryn, which means "of the Rhine."

The Calvinist states of the northern Netherlands had recently won their independence from the Roman Catholic Habsburg rule in the south, and Leiden, which was traditionally the residence of the counts of Holland, became an intellectual and cultural center of the Reformation when it was endowed with a university by William of Orange in recognition of the citizens' successful resistance to the Spanish. Rembrandt enrolled as a student of literature at this university in 1620, but as his real talent was for drawing he left the university in 1621 to be apprenticed for three years to an obscure artist called Jakob van Swanenburgh. In 1624 he was sent to Amsterdam to study with Pieter Lastman. He remained with Lastman only six months, yet this master's style influenced his work for many years.

Rembrandt returned home in 1625 and shared a studio with his friend Jan Lievens. His early work shows the strong influence of Caravaggio, whose style was well known at Utrecht among a group of followers. Rembrandt's mother had instilled in him a knowledge and love of the Bible, and Biblical themes were to be

Self-portrait, about 1634
Florence, Pal. Pitti

Self-portrait at the Age of 34, 1640
London, N. G.

David Playing his Harp before Saul, about 1657
The Hague, Mauritshuis

Self-portrait, about 1660
London, Kenwood House, Iveagh Bequest

93

Woman Bathing in a Stream, 1655
London, N. G.

among his favorite subjects, enabling him to indulge his love of the exotic and picturesque. At this time Rembrandt began the collection of "stage props" with which he embellished his pictures.

Since the Reformation the demand for church paintings had ceased, and the chapels and cloisters were occupied by municipal groups. These citizens were among the chief patrons of artists and had already established a tradition of group portraiture. In 1632 Rembrandt was commissioned by the Amsterdam guild of surgeons to paint a group portrait. His careful arrangement of the composition, *The Anatomy Lesson of Dr. Tulp*, which gave prominence to each member of the group without seeming contrived or unnatural, and his sympathetic rendering of the actual portraits, revealed a skill in collective character portrayal that had never been achieved before. Soon the rich and the fashionable flooded Rembrandt with commissions for portraits. Prince Frederik Hendrik was one of his patrons.

Among Rembrandt's sitters was Saskia van Uylenborch, a young lady of an aristocratic family. Rembrandt and Saskia became engaged, and were married as soon as she came of age in 1634. Saskia's large dowry and his own impulsive love of collecting beautiful objects and paintings soon tempted him to live beyond his means. In 1639 Rembrandt bought a large house, using as the initial deposit loans from relatives and friends. He was unable to pay the remainder in the time stipulated; the accumulated interest on this debt caused his financial ruin.

He continued to paint many portraits of Saskia, often in exotic costumes. He had more applications from would-be apprentices from all over Holland and neighboring countries than he could accept. He set his pupils to work in individual cubicles so that they would not be distracted or influenced by each other's efforts.

Meanwhile Saskia, taxed by the births of three children, none of whom survived,

Rembrandt

The Night Watch, 1642
Amsterdam, Rijksmus.

Bathsheba, 1654
Paris, Louvre

94

died in 1644 only a year after the birth of her fourth child, Titus. Rembrandt made an eloquent series of drawings and etchings, which depict the pathetic decline of a young, healthy girl into a pitiful bedridden invalid. The year of Saskia's death, 1644, was the beginning of the decline in Rembrandt's fortunes. In 1642 he had produced his famous painting now known as *The Night Watch*. It was unpopular with its subjects because equal prominence was not given to each of the sitters, and they had arranged to share the artist's fee in equal amounts. Subsequently the composition, which Rembrandt had considered more important than the original intention of a group portrait, was damaged by clumsy trimming when it was moved to the Amsterdam Town Hall, where "it was found necessary to cut off two figures to the right of the canvas, and part of the drum to the right to fit it into its allotted space." By the 18th century the painting had become so darkened by grime and smoke that it came to be known as *The Night Watch*, although cleaning has shown it to be a scene full of light and color.

After this incident Rembrandt's popularity somewhat declined, but several important friends and art lovers, including Prince Frederik Hendrik, still appreciated his work and continued to encourage him with several commissions for which they paid record sums, even exceeding the price previously paid by the prince for a painting by Rubens. In spite of this help, Rembrandt's financial troubles increased. Nevertheless his style developed. The elements of rhetoric disappeared and he found a way to express deep intimate human feeling.

From 1645 Rembrandt lived with his servant, Hendrickje Stoffels, who often acted as his model. This caused a public scandal and Hendrickje was admonished by the church elders. Three months later she gave birth to a daughter, Cornelia.

By 1653, Rembrandt owed 8400 florins, and became involved in complicated legal proceedings to protect Titus' share of his mother's legacy from creditors. One of his most prolific years was 1656, in which he worked hard to meet his debts. Nevertheless, in July of that year he was declared bankrupt, and his belongings were sold between 1657 and 1660 for a ridiculously small sum.

Titus provided for both his father and Hendrickje and also for his half sister

The Incredulity of Thomas, 1634
Leningrad, Hermitage

The Entombment, about 1659
London, B. M.

The Last Supper, 1635 (after Leonardo da Vinci)
West Berlin, Staatl. Mus.

Cornelia from his inheritance. Eventually Titus and Hendrickje set up an art dealer's business and "employed" Rembrandt as an "adviser," thus protecting him from his creditors and freeing him from worry. He was once again able to concentrate on his work. As his sight deteriorated in his old age he produced fewer etchings and used a palette knife for broader effects in his paintings. He still received some important commissions, and he continued his magnificent series of self-portraits, which show him at every stage from hopeful youth to a disillusioned but indomitable old age. He died in 1669. His influence was immense in his own day and has never faded.

Ed. A. Bredius   The Paintings of Rembrandt   London, 1937
Ludwig Münz   Rembrandt's Etchings, Vols I and II   London, 1952
Henry Dumont   Rembrandt   The Hague, 1955
T. Copplestone   Rembrandt   London, 1960

The Raising of the Cross, about 1655-60
West Berlin, Staatl. Mus.

Christ Carrying the Cross, about 1650
Haarlem, Teyler's Mus.

The Entombment, about 1658
Haarlem, Teyler's Mus.

SUZE ROBERTSON   1855-1922

A painter of the late Dutch Impressionist school

Suze Robertson was born in 1855 at The Hague. She studied at the Academy between 1874 and 1877, years which also marked George Hendrik Breitner's period
there. She later attended the Amsterdam Academy, where she was a pupil of
August Allebé. After returning to The Hague she married the painter Richard
Bisschop in 1890.

She painted chiefly town views and figures. Though she is generally considered
to be one of the Amsterdam Impressionists, her work is more nearly expressionist
because of its subject-matter and because the role of light in her pictures is less
important than in impressionist works. Her painting is characterized by the dark
but glowing colors with which she gives her simple subjects a sense of the implicit
tragedy of life. Anticipating Dutch Expressionism as it does, her work recalls that
of Paula Modersohn-Becker and, especially in the drawings of women, the work of
Käthe Kollwitz. Suze Robertson died in 1922.

HER WORKS INCLUDE
The White House, about 1893
Otterlo, Holland, Kröller-Müller
Peasant Woman at the Oven,
about 1895
Otterlo, Holland, Kröller-Müller
Girl Putting on her Shoe
Otterlo, Holland, Kröller-Müller
Evening Landscape
Otterlo, Holland, Kröller-Müller

See also page 244

FÉLICIEN ROPS   1833-1898

An artist who worked principally in the graphic medium

Félicien Rops was born in Namur, Belgium, on July 7, 1833. His childhood was
spent in Namur, but he later went to Brussels. While studying at Brussels University he helped produce "Crocodile," a student magazine. His illustrations attracted
the attention of some publishers, who offered him commissions, among them the
design for a cover of works by the 18th-century English poet John Hay.

In 1845, after his father died, he built a studio in the garden of the house where
his mother was living. With the help of friends, he trained himself as an artist.
During 1859 and 1860 he went to Paris, where he worked in the studio of Henri
Jacquemart. On his return to Brussels he founded the International Society of
Etchers, which proved to be short-lived; he thereafter frequently left Brussels to
paint and draw in the Ardennes and the Campine. Gustave Courbet, during a visit
to Belgium, met him, but appears not to have taken him seriously, although *The
Absinthe Drinker*, 1865, proved Rops to be one of the foremost graphic artists of
Belgium. In style he presents some parallels to both Honoré Daumier and Paul
Gavarni. His subject-matter was varied, including many studies of young girls. In
later years he became increasingly interested in etching.

After 1874 Rops settled in Paris, and spent most of his time producing book
illustrations, which included designs for works by Théophile Gautier, Voltaire,
and Stéphane Mallarmé. He also executed many oil paintings in a style close to
that of Courbet, and did various pen-and-ink sketches. He brought out a volume
entitled "One Hundred Sketches to Delight Solid Citizens," and he joined Les XX.
His last work was the design for an advertisement of an exhibition. Rops died in
1898 at Essonnes, Seine-et-Oise.

The Quarrel, 1877
Brussels, Mus. Royaux des B-A.

HIS WORKS INCLUDE
Val du Colombier near Namur, 1875
Paris, Louvre
Lady with a Lamp, 1876
London, V. and A.
Landscape in the Ardennes
Antwerp, Mus. Royal des B-A.
The Beach
Brussels, Mus. Royaux des B-A.

See also pages 200, 241

Self-portrait, about 1640
Vienna, Kunsthist. Mus.

Pietro Paulo Rubens

HIS WORKS INCLUDE

The Crowning with Thorns, 1602
Grasse, France, Hôpital du Petit-Paris

The Circumcision, about 1605
Vienna, Gemäldegal.

The Transfiguration, about 1606
Nancy, France, Mus. des B-A.

St. Gregory and St. Domitilla,
about 1608
Grenoble, France, Mus. des B-A.

The Toilet of Venus, about 1613
Vienna, Gall. Liechtenstein

The Deposition, about 1615
Leningrad, Hermitage

The Last Communion of St. Francis
1619
Antwerp, Mus. Royal des B-A.

The Assumption of the Virgin, 1626
Antwerp, Cathedral

The Mystic Marriage of St. Catherine
1628
Antwerp, Cathedral

Neptune Stilling the Tempest,
about 1635
Cambridge, Mass., Fogg Art Mus.

Peasant Dancer, about 1637
Madrid, Prado

The Madonna with Saints, about 1640
Antwerp, St. Jacques

**See also pages 153, 154, 155, 156,
157, 223 ,224, 225, 226**

A diplomat and Flemish Baroque painter of genius

The circumstances of Peter Paul Rubens' birth were kept secret by his mother even from Rubens himself, in order to cover up his father's infidelities with the wife of William of Orange and his subsequent punishment and imprisonment at Siegen in Germany. It is thought, however, that Rubens was born in Siegen in 1577.

After educating him along humanistic lines in Cologne and Antwerp, his mother, recognizing his talent for drawing, arranged for him to be apprenticed to her relative Tobias Verhaecht, a landscape painter. Later Rubens joined the studio of Adam van Noort, a painter in the Flemish tradition, where he was a fellow pupil of Jacob Jordaens. After four years there he left to join the studio of Otto van Veen. This new master was a cultured and highly esteemed painter in the Romanist tradition, patronized by the aristocracy. In 1598, before leaving his studio, Rubens was admitted to the Antwerp painters' guild. Meanwhile he assisted van Veen with decorations for the ceremonial entry of the Archduke Albert and the Infanta Isabella into Brussels. The young painter may have met his future patron, Vincenzo Gonzaga, the Duke of Mantua, at these festivities.

In 1600 Rubens went to Italy. In Venice the wonderful coloring of Titian,

The Raising of the Cross, about 1620
Paris, Louvre

Tintoretto, and Veronese permanently affected his own use of color. It was while Rubens was in northern Italy that the Duke of Mantua engaged him as his court painter. At this illustrious court Rubens studied the duke's extensive collection of paintings and antique sculpture, some of which considerably influenced his art. The duke's famous stables and menagerie, which contained tigers, crocodiles, and other exotic creatures, made a lasting impression on Rubens. Drawings of these animals were later incorporated into his hunting scenes.

In 1603 Rubens was entrusted by the duke with a diplomatic mission to Philip III of Spain. His contact with the painters and artists of Madrid and its environs further broadened his outlook. While there he executed many portraits, among them an equestrian portrait of the Duke of Lerma.

In 1601 and again in 1606 Rubens visited Rome, where he found a new patron in Scipione Borghese, the nephew of the pope and the future patron of the sculptor Gian Lorenzo Bernini. In Rome he executed an altarpiece for the Church of S. Maria in Vallicella, *The Madonna with Angels*. He was dissatisfied with this first version, which was later erected over his mother's tomb in Antwerp. The second version, still in the church for which it was commissioned, is in three separate parts. It is interesting in that the subject-matter, distributed over three sections, is linked emotionally into one whole, an early example of a spatial continuity that was to reach its culmination in the High Baroque style.

In 1608, hearing that his mother was dying, Rubens left Italy for Antwerp. On arriving there he was almost immediately appointed court painter to the Infanta Isabella and the Archduke Ferdinand. The next year he married Isabella Brandt, daughter of an Antwerp scholar.

One of Rubens' first commissions on his return to Antwerp was for an altarpiece for the cathedral. With the payment for this he built himself a palatial home, with studios and accommodation for his flock of apprentices. The design of the building and surrounding gardens is somewhat reminiscent in style of the palace at Mantua.

The Triumph of Truth: from the History of Maria de' Medici, about 1622-25
Paris, Louvre

Christ's Charge to Peter, about 1616
London, Wallace Coll.

The Adoration of the Magi, about 1625
London, Wallace Coll.

The Holy Family with Elizabeth and St. John the Baptist, about 1616
London, Wallace Coll.

Isabella Brandt, about 1615-20
London, Wallace Coll.

It was in this palatial home that Rubens executed commissions from all over Europe, including orders from the Holy Roman Emperor, Philip III of Spain, James I of England, and the king of Poland. He was able to achieve an enormous output by organizing his workshop on a production-line system. He would hand to assistants a preliminary sketch in pale non-committal colors, which they would enlarge on to canvas, painting in the masses. Rubens himself would then add the finishing touches, color, and detail in his own inimitable hand. He also made drawings to be engraved as book illustrations. Among his assistants were Anthony van Dyck, Jacob Jordaens, and Frans Snyders. He also collaborated with the flower painter Jan Bruegel the Elder.

Until 1620 two styles had alternated in Rubens' work, a pictorial one derived from Italian sources, such as Titian, Tintoretto, and Veronese, and a more classical manner consisting of considered compositions and cool colors. In 1620 he was commissioned to decorate the ceiling of the Jesuit church in Antwerp. Unfortunately burned down a century later, it was the first ceiling in northern Europe to be decorated with superimposed canvases in the Venetian manner. 15 years afterward, in England, Rubens executed for Charles I the ceiling decoration of the Banqueting Hall, Whitehall, London, in the same manner. Meanwhile he made

The Judgment of Paris, about 1632
London, N. G.

several visits to Paris at the request of Maria de' Medici, for whom he executed extensive decorations for the Luxembourg Palace.

In 1626 Isabella Brandt died. Four years later Rubens married his second wife, Helena Fourment, the 16-year-old daughter of a wealthy silk merchant. She became the theme and inspiration of his late mythologies and the subject of many of his portraits.

Rubens passed his remaining years as a country gentleman on the estates of the Château of Steen at Elleweert. Despite this semi-retirement from the world, he received commissions as a painter and diplomat until the end of his life in 1640. During this time he also painted landscapes, particularly of the countryside around his château.

M. Rooses Rubens London, 1904
E. Dillon Rubens London, 1909
W. R. Valentenir The Art of the Low Countries New York, 1914
J. A. Goris and J. Held Rubens in America New York, 1947
L. van Puyvelde The Sketches of Rubens London, 1947
R. S. Magurn The Letters of P. P. Rubens Cambridge, Mass., 1955
J. Held Rubens, Selected Drawings London, 1959
H. Gerson and E. H. ter Kuile Art and Architecture in Belgium 1600–1800 London, 1960

Portrait of Helena Fourment,
about 1630
Monaco, Mus. Nat. des B-A.

The Feast of Venus, about 1632
Vienna, Kunsthist. Mus.

An Old Oak, about 1650
London, N. G.

JAKOB VAN RUISDAEL

about 1628-1682

A landscape painter known especially for his rendering of trees

Jakob van Ruisdael was born in Haarlem, probably in 1628, and his father was a framemaker who may also have been a painter. It seems likely that he became a pupil of his uncle, Salomon van Ruysdael, who painted landscapes of some merit, and perhaps also of Hendrik Cornelisz Vroom. He lived in Haarlem until about 1655 and then moved to Amsterdam, ultimately returning to Haarlem, where he died in 1682.

The earliest date that appears on any of van Ruisdael's pictures is 1646. In 1648 he became a member of the Guild of St. Luke in his native town, and in 1659 was made a freeman of the city of Amsterdam. His paintings show that he was familiar with the scenery of most of Holland and also of some of the nearer parts of Germany. He enjoyed no great reputation while he was alive—a fact that is surprising in view of the high regard in which he was later to be held.

To judge from the works of Ruisdael's contemporaries, the Biblical or mythological picture, the portrait, and the scene of domestic or village life may have had a greater appeal to potential buyers than his somewhat somber landscapes, however beautifully conceived and painted. This is probably the explanation of Ruisdael's

An Extensive Landscape (detail) about 1670
London, N. G.

lack of success, since in his own field he is clearly a master. The human figure is a rarity in his work, and where figures are introduced they are thought to be the work of either Adriaen van de Velde or Philips Wouwerman.

Landscape was van Ruisdael's love, and his many pictures of the countryside prove the excellence of his technique. He was fully capable of creating a feeling of tenderness and romance. Superb cloud-covered skies spread with a magnificent threat over many of his landscapes.

Van Ruisdael was also fond of peaceful woodland scenery, and is considered to be one of the finest painters of trees. Some of his pictures show mountains, indicating that he probably traveled at some time in his life. Scenes of the sea and shore come within his oeuvre. His paintings of waterfalls are believed to be directly influenced by those of the painter Allart van Everdingen, who visited Scandinavia in 1640 and introduced this new style of romantic mountain landscape into Holland. There is also a painting of Haarlem seen from a distance, now in a private collection.

Van Ruisdael is thought to have painted well over 1000 pictures. Nearly every major museum has one, but the best collection is in the National Gallery, London.

N. Maclaren   The Dutch School, N. G. Catalogue   London, 1960

Watermill, about 1652
London, N. G.

HIS WORKS INCLUDE

Forest Scene, 1653
Amsterdam, Rijksmus.

View of Amsterdam, about 1660
Budapest, Mus. of Fine Arts

Oak Wood, about 1660
West Berlin, Staatl. Mus.

The Burst of Sunlight, about 1670
Paris, Louvre

Mill near Wijk bij Duurstede, about 1670
Amsterdam, Rijksmus.

See also pages 187, 236

PIETER SAENREDAM   1597-1665

A painter of church interiors

Pieter Saenredam was born in 1597, son of the engraver Jan Saenredam. After 1612 he was a pupil of Frans de Grebber in Haarlem, where he was to work for most of his life and where he died in 1665. His travels took him to Assendelft, 's Hertogenbosch, Rhenen, Amsterdam, Alkmaar, and Utrecht.

Saenredam's work consists mostly of church interiors in cool, silvery tones that impart a sense of hallowed silence. He revived in the 17th century this typically Dutch genre. Together with Gerrit Berckheyde and Emmanuel de Witte, Saenredam arrived at a realistic rendering of architecture, as opposed to the visionary and idealized paintings of the Neefs, the van Steenwijks, and Vredeman de Vries in the 16th century. There are many elaborate preparatory drawings from Saenredam's works that have a value of their own. In some of Saenredam's works the figures are by Adriaen van Ostade and Jan Both. Saenredam possessed the sketch book of Maerten van Heemskerk, from which he used drawings for his two views of Rome.

N. Maclaren   The Dutch School, N. G. Catalogue   London, 1960

P'Soenredam.

Interior of the Grote Kerk at Haarlem, 1637   *London, N. G.*

HIS WORKS INCLUDE

Interior of the Church of St. Mary, Utrecht, 1641
Amsterdam, Rijksmus.

Interior of the Church of Assendelft, 1649
Amsterdam, Rijksmus.

Interior of the Church of St. Cunera, Rhenen, 1655
The Hague, Mauritshuis

Old Town Hall of Amsterdam, 1657
Amsterdam, Rijksmus.

See also pages 180, 230

Company of Farmers
Amsterdam, Rijksmus.

HIS WORKS INCLUDE

The Annunciation to the Shepherds
Amsterdam, Rijksmus.

See also page 234

CORNELIUS SAFTLEVEN 1607-1681

A highly competent graphic artist

Cornelius Saftleven was born in 1607 in Gorkum in Holland. His first teacher was his brother, who himself had been the pupil of Jan van Goyen. Saftleven worked principally in Rotterdam, where he twice married, and where he became the dean of the painters' guild in 1667. He traveled to Antwerp and Utrecht in 1635. He died in Rotterdam in 1681.

Saftleven is chiefly famous as a graphic artist, although his etchings are rare. His drawings of animals, many of which survive, show great competence. The influence of Hercules Seghers is clear in Saftleven's style. He also knew the work of Rubens, with whom he collaborated for a time, and that of Adriaen Brouwer and David Teniers the Younger. Saftleven's works are often satirical, and he also executed religious themes and landscapes.

Elijah Being Fed by the Ravens, 1634
Amsterdam, Rijksmus.

HIS WORKS INCLUDE

Interior of a Cow Stall, 1615
Amsterdam, Rijksmus.
Stag Hunt in a Rocky Landscape, 1620
Amsterdam, Rijksmus.
Orpheus, 1628
London, N. G.

See also page 223

ROELANT SAVERY about 1576-1639

A painter of animals and flowers

Roelant Savery was born, probably in 1576, in Courtrai in Flanders. According to Karel van Mander, Savery was for a time the pupil of his elder brother Jacob. His work also shows the influence of Gillis van Coninxloo, who settled in Amsterdam. As a young man Savery probably lived in Amsterdam. From 1604 until 1615 he also worked at The Hague and in Vienna.

There are no pictures by Roelant Savery dated before 1602. Within a few years of that date he began a period of traveling and working for various royal patrons. It is known that by 1605 he was in Prague in the service of Emperor Rudolph II. Rudolph sent Savery for two years to the Tyrol, probably from 1606 to 1608, in order to draw the landscape. The emperor died in 1612 and Savery apparently returned to Amsterdam the following year, but by September, 1614, he was under the patronage of Emperor Matthias in Vienna.

Savery painted landscapes, which almost invariably represented the Garden of Eden, or depicted Orpheus among the animals. He was one of the first Dutch painters to produce pictures with animals as the main subject. There are also flower paintings by his hand. In addition to his many paintings, he produced a number of etchings.

Savery returned to Holland after only a short period in Vienna, for by January, 1616, he was again in Amsterdam. Three years later he had settled in Utrecht, and entered the painters' guild. He remained in Utrecht until his death in 1639.

I. Bergström *Still-life Painting in the 17th Century* London, *1916*
K. van Mander *Het Schilderboek* Haarlem, *1604 (English translation in C. van der Wall
Dutch and Flemish Painters New York, 1936)*

JAN VAN SCOREL

1495-1562

A much traveled artist who was influenced by the 16th-century Italian manner

Jan van Scorel, born in 1495, is named after his birthplace, a small town near Alkmaar, Holland. He was a pupil of Cornelis Cornelisz Buys in Alkmaar, and later of Jakob Cornelius Oostanen in Amsterdam. He also studied under Jan Gossaert, called Mabuse, in Utrecht.

In 1519 van Scorel traveled to Cologne to study architecture and perspective, and to Nuremberg, where he visited Albrecht Dürer. The following year he was in Styria and Carinthia painting an altarpiece in Obervellach Parish Church. He then moved on to Venice, where he absorbed the influence of Giorgione and Palma Vecchio. In Venice he met a Dutch churchman who persuaded him to go to Jerusalem on a pilgrimage. He was entertained by the Superior of the Monastery of Sion, who acted as his guide to the Holy City, and suggested subjects for his sketchbook. In return, van Scorel painted for his host *The Incredulity of St. Thomas*, incorporating scenes of Jerusalem. On the journey back to Italy, he made drawings in the island of Rhodes. Van Scorel reached Rome in 1522, during the pontificate of the Dutch pope, Hadrian VI, who gave his compatriot a commission to paint his portrait. The pope also appointed him Inspector of the Belvedere, which then, as now, housed the famous Vatican collection of antique sculpture.

At about this time, van Scorel was much influenced by his great contemporary

The Good Samaritan, 1537
Amsterdam, Rijksmus.

Christ's Entry into Jerusalem, about 1527
Utrecht, Centraal Mus. der Gemeente

Michelangelo, and by Raphael who had recently died. Before dying in 1524, Pope Hadrian made van Scorel Canon of Utrecht. On his return to Utrecht, van Scorel lived with the dean of the minster and painted for Utrecht Cathedral his masterpiece, *Christ's Entry into Jerusalem.* In 1540 he visited France, and in 1550 he was asked to restore van Eyck's altarpiece in the Cathedral of St. Bavon in Ghent.

Much of van Scorel's work was destroyed by the iconoclasts of the 16th century. Among his pupils were Maerten van Heemskerk and Anthonis Mor. The latter painted a picture to hang over his master's tomb when he died in Utrecht in 1562.

E. G. Troche   Painting in the Netherlands in the 15th and 16th Centuries   London, 1936

River in a Valley (detail) about 1620
Amsterdam, Rijksmus.

HERCULES SEGHERS   1589/90 - about 1638

An experimental etcher and painter of mountain scenery

Hercules Seghers was born in 1589/90, probably in Haarlem, but very little is known of his life. He was a pupil of the Flemish landscape painter Gillis van Coninxloo. He was an almost exact contemporary of Gerard van Honthorst, and about 16 years older than Rembrandt.

Seghers seems first to have lived and taught in Haarlem, but in 1614 he went to live in Amsterdam. In 1631 he was in Utrecht, and in 1633 at The Hague. His surviving works distinguish him sharply from most of the Dutch painters of the time, in that they frequently show mountain scenery, usually without figures. There is no record of his having visited Switzerland, but there is every indication that he knew the Alps and was greatly impressed by their grandeur and their height.

Seghers was an etcher of great skill, and because of his experiments may be considered a reviver of the art of etching. He frequently used colored paper or tinted the proofs to achieve romantic and dramatic effects. Rembrandt was a great admirer of his works and owned a number of them. In his lifetime Seghers did not appeal to a large public, but the great artists saw the significance of this solitary man. He died in 1638 or possibly earlier.

N. Maclaren   The Dutch School, N. G. Catalogue   London, 1960

A Mountainous Landscape
London, N. G.

CLAUS SLUTER

active about 1380-1406

A sculptor independent of the prevalent International Gothic style

Claus Sluter was born in Holland, although very little is known of his antecedents. He settled in Dijon, where he worked for the Duke of Burgundy. It is probable that he had worked in Brussels before replacing the Fleming Jean de Marville, who died in 1389, as supervisor of the sculptures for the Chartreuse de Champmol, near Dijon. Sluter must have had a considerable reputation when he arrived in Dijon, because he was made a *valet de chambre*, had a large house near the castle, and set up his own workshop. When he died his nephew and pupil, Claus de Werve, succeeded to his position. It is known that Sluter made two journeys, one to the Netherlands and one to Paris, to obtain marble and alabaster.

Sluter worked on sculptures for the Chartreuse, and finished the decorations of its doorway, probably begun by Marville. The decorations included the figures of *St. Catherine* and *St. John*, finished in 1391, and that of *Margaret, Duchess of Burgundy*, two years later. This work was interrupted by another commission, *The Well of Moses*, which was decorated with six full-length figures of prophets. Originally this was crowned by a great Calvary, together with the figures of the Virgin Mary, St. Mary Magdalen, St. John, and weeping angels.

Sluter worked on the tomb of Philip the Bold, which was completed after his death by Claus de Werve. The figures of mourners around the tomb are simple and dramatic, with thick drapes very different from those produced by the conventions of the prevalent International Gothic style. This type of sepulchral sculpture spread far beyond France. Sluter's work represented a completely new development in the art of northern Europe, and was to exercise a considerable influence on the artists of his day. He departed from the accepted Gothic conventions and evolved a new realistic style in which the sense of movement and vigor had no counterpart among contemporary sculptors.

Mourner: from the Tomb of Philip the Bold, about 1404
Dijon, France, Musée des B-A.

HIS WORKS INCLUDE

Head of Christ: from the Calvary, 1399
Dijon, France, Chartreuse de Champmol
The Well of Moses, 1395-1404
Dijon, France, Chartreuse de Champmol

See also pages 258, 259

Jeremiah (detail): from the Well of Moses, 1395-1404
Dijon, France, Chartreuse de Champmol

Mourner: from the Tomb of Philip the Bold, about 1404
Dijon, France, Musée des B-A.

JAKOB SMITS   1856-1928

A painter concerned with the effects of light in landscape

Born in Rotterdam, Smits studied at the academies of Rotterdam, Brussels, and Munich, and traveled to Vienna, Rome, and London. In 1889 he settled in Achterbosch, near Mol, in Belgium, becoming a naturalized Belgian in 1902. His was a simple, strong, peasant art. Using a pigment that was thick and granulated, he rendered the effects of light in the Campine landscape within a firmly disciplined composition. He made much use of deep colors on a gold-yellow background.

Self-portrait
Vienna, Kunsthist. Mus.

BARTHOLOMEUS SPRANGER   1546 - after 1627

A much traveled Flemish painter, engraver, and sculptor

Bartholomeus Spranger was born in Antwerp on March 21, 1546, the son of an Antwerp merchant, Joachim Spranger. He showed an early interest in painting, and was the pupil of Jan Mandyn in Haarlem in 1557. He later worked with Frans Mostaert and Cornelis van Dalem.

Spranger traveled widely during his career. At some time about 1565 he was working in Paris. From there he traveled to Lyons, and then to Italy, where he visited Milan and Parma before going on to Rome. For three years he worked on the Villa Farnese in Caprarola for Cardinal Farnese, and later he was employed by Pope Pius V.

Spranger's work in Rome was completed by 1575, and he moved to Vienna, where he was employed by Emperor Maximilian II, who made him his court painter. This post continued under Rudolph, whom Spranger accompanied to Augsburg in 1582, after visiting Prague. In 1584 he was made painter to the imperial chamber, and four years later was given a patent of nobility. Spranger returned to the Netherlands in 1602, and was fêted by the Haarlem artists and entertained by Karel van Mander. In addition to producing paintings of religious and mythological subjects, he worked as a sculptor and also made prints.

The Town Planners, 1893
Brussels, Parc du Cinquantenaire

KAREL VAN DER STAPPEN   1843-1910

A sculptor, medalist, and decorator

Karel van der Stappen was born in Brussels in December, 1843. He studied with Jean François Portaels at the Brussels Academy, became a teacher there in 1883, and was later made director. His allegorical group, *The Birth of Crime*, was refused at the Brussels Salon in 1863, but was accepted three years later.

Van der Stappen spent some time traveling in Europe. In 1871 he visited Florence and he stayed in Rome during 1876 and the following three years, after which he went to Paris. When he returned to Belgium he executed statues and decorations for various buildings in Brussels. These comprise almost his entire output. He designed an allegorical bronze group, *Aspiration to Art,* for the façade of the Musées Royaux des Beaux-Arts, and made for the Great Hall of the same building two bronze figures, *Greek Art* and *Gothic Art.* At the Place de la Justice was placed his statue of *Alex Gendebien,* a portrait of a member of the provisional government in 1830. In 1893 Stappen's bronze group, *The Town Planners,* was set up in the Parc du Cinquantenaire. His most important commission was the *Monument to Human Labor* for the provisional council of Brabant.

HIS WORKS INCLUDE

The Sphinx, 1898
Brussels, Mus. Royaux des B-A.
The Town Planners, 1893
Brussels, Parc du Cinquantenaire
Aspiration to Art
Brussels, Mus. Royaux des B-A.
A Pair of Wrestlers
Brussels, Rond-Point de l'Avenue Louise

See also page 280

JAN STEEN   1626-1679

A prolific artist of tavern scenes and Dutch bourgeois life

Jan Steen was born in 1626, the son of a brewer in Leiden. He may have attended the famous university there, possibly as a student of literature. His first study of painting was under the German artist Nicholas Knupfer, but he then joined the studio of Jan van Goyen, whose daughter he married in 1649. Like Jan Vermeer, he became a member of the Guild of St. Luke, moving to The Hague in 1649 and to Delft five years later.

Steen lived in Haarlem from soon after 1660 until 1671. He opened a tavern in Leiden in 1671, a year after marrying his second wife, the daughter of a bookseller. He died in Leiden in 1679, and it is said that he left as many as 500 pictures unsold.

Self-portrait
Amsterdam, Rijksmus.

The Lute-player (detail)
London, Wallace Coll.

A Peasant Family at Meal-time:
"Grace before Meat," about 1665
London, N. G.

Young Woman Playing the Harpsichord
about 1659
London, N. G.

In many ways Steen was the perfect embodiment of Dutch painting in the mid-17th century. He was fascinated by the *bourgeoisie* and the lower middle class, generally avoiding the aristocrat and even the cultured man, although he occasionally painted the rich and respectable in their homes. His pictures, however, only came to life when he painted tavern scenes, sometimes looking at them with a keenly satirical eye, sometimes with the sympathy that might be expected from the little that is known of him.

There are not many portraits by Jan Steen, but, in common with nearly all Dutch painters, he executed a number of religious pictures, some of them on a large scale. These were less successful than his favorite depictions of tavern scenes and of the life of the small business man and shopkeeper. He produced a well-known series of pictures showing the visits of a doctor to a young woman patient. Chemists in their workshops provided another characteristic theme. He also executed many scenes of marriage festivities and card parties, the same models frequently appearing in different paintings. What distinguished Steen from other Dutch painters of similar subjects was the beauty of his coloring, the sureness of his draftmanship, and the touch of drama he so often re-created.

ALFRED STEVENS   1823-1906

A painter of Parisian elegance during the Second Empire

Alfred Stevens was born on May 11, 1823, in Brussels. He there studied under the painter François Joseph Navez, the director of the Brussels Academy. Stevens' father, an officer in the service of the king of the Netherlands, was a friend of the boy's next master, the French painter Camille Roqueplan. Stevens went to Paris to study with Roqueplan in 1844, and also attended classes at the École des Beaux-Arts, where Jean Auguste Dominique Ingres was a professor at the time. After several years Stevens went back to Brussels, but in 1849 he returned to Paris. There he established himself, and he began to exhibit at the Salon, for it was in Paris that he found the material for most of his paintings. He painted a cross-section of contemporary life, depicting fashionable society in many elegant compositions and portraits. His genre scenes and his paintings of Parisiennes provided a record of life under the Second Empire. He was also one of the first European painters to be inspired by Japanese art.

In 1855 Stevens exhibited at the Antwerp Salon a small picture entitled *At Home;* he had already shown some work in the Paris Exhibition of 1853. In the Exhibition of 1867 he had a number of his paintings on display, and from that time participated in all the large exhibitions, including the Paris International Exhibition of 1889 and the Exhibition of Belgian Art in Brussels in 1880.

After 1890 Stevens exhibited regularly with the Société Nationale des Beaux-Arts. In 1886 he published his "Impressions of Painting," which was an immediate success and was translated into several languages.

DAVID TENIERS the YOUNGER

Flemish painter of genre subjects

David Teniers the Younger was born in Antwerp. First trained by his father, David Teniers the Elder (1582-1649), who had studied under Rubens, he soon came under the influence of the Dutch genre painter Adriaen Brouwer. Typical works of this early period are *The Prodigal Son* and *The Five Senses*. Teniers became a master in the guild of St. Luke in 1632/3, and in 1637 he married Anne Bruegel, daughter of Jan (Velvet) Bruegel.

After Brouwer's death in 1638, Teniers developed his own style. He produced his best work during the period 1640-50, with monumental processions like *The Meeting of the Civic Guards* and open landscapes with scenes of village revelry such as *The Village Fête*. In 1651 he moved to Brussels, where he was employed by the archduke Leopold Wilhelm, Regent of the Netherlands, both as painter and keeper of his collection. He made many copies of works in the collection under the title « Theatrum Pictorium ». His paintings of entire galleries provide an invaluable inventory of the collections. The quality of Teniers' art began to decline after about 1650, and many of his later commissions were probably executed by assistants. In 1663 he helped to found the Academy at Brussels.

Teniers was a prolific painter of a great variety of subjects, but he is chiefly known for his pictures of peasant life, rustic interiors, tavern scenes, and the like, which had an important influence on the development of Flemish genre painting in the 18th century.

His son David (1638-85) was also a painter of considerable ability.

HIS WORKS INCLUDE

The Barn, 1634
Karlsruhe, Staatl. Kunsthalle

The Five Senses, about 1634
Brussels, Mus. des B-A.

The Meeting of the Civic Guards, 1643
Leningrad, Hermitage

The Kitchen, 1644
The Hague, Mauritshuis

The Picture Gallery of Archduke Leopold Wilhelm of Austria, about 1654
Madrid, Prado

D·TENIERS·F·

The Prodigal Son, about 1635
Munich, Alte Pin.

The Village Fête, 1643
London, N. G.

The Meeting of the Civic Guards, 1643
Leningrad, Hermitage

The Theorbo Lesson, about 1670
London, N. G.

HIS WORKS INCLUDE

The Dispatch, 1653
The Hague, Mauritshuis

Visitors, before 1655
Amsterdam, Rijksmus.

Portrait of Old Men Standing,
about 1660
West Berlin, Staatl. Mus.

The Gallant, about 1665
Paris, Louvre

A Glass of Lemonade
Leningrad, Hermitage

The Suitor's Visit
Washington, D. C., N. G., Mellon Coll.

See also page 172

Portrait of a Young Man, about 1665
London, N. G.

GERARD TERBORCH   1617-1681

A skilled genre painter and portrayer of the Dutch aristocracy

Gerard Terborch was born at Zwolle in the northern Netherlands in 1617, the son of a tax collector who was also a painter. He came from a wealthier family than most of the Dutch artists of his time and evidently had the means to travel extensively. He was therefore not forced to compete with the rather overwhelming talent all around him, and had the opportunity to earn a good living by painting portraits abroad. Moreover, his family appear to have provided him with plenty of introductions, and he passed his life in circumstances and surroundings more elegant than those open to most of his contemporaries.

Terborch was in Amsterdam in 1632 and two years later became a pupil in the studio of Pieter Moulijn at Haarlem. In 1635 he went to London, and in 1641 he traveled to Rome, where he painted some portraits, including *Jan Six* and *A Young Lady*, both small-scale works. In 1648 he went to Münster, where the peace conference was being held, and in that year painted *The Peace of Münster*. One of the portraits in this picture is of the Count of Peneranda, the Spanish plenipotentiary at the peace conference, who invited Terborch to Madrid.

Terborch accepted this invitation in 1648, and while in Madrid is said to have painted the king of Spain, Philip IV. Diego Velázquez was in Madrid at that time,

The Peace of Münster, 1648
London, N. G.

and the influence he had on Terborch is clear in the latter's *Portrait of a Young Man*, which has all the courtliness and grace of a typical Velázquez portrait. Instead of being lifesize, however, it measures only 26 by 21 inches.

In 1650 Terborch returned to Holland. He married in 1654 and lived for the rest of his life in Deventer, dying there in 1681. In Deventer he enjoyed great success as a portrait painter. It seems certain that his likenesses were excellent, although endowed with a dignity and distinction that may well have flattered his sitters. Most of them are on a very small scale, and so would look well in the intimacy of a well-to-do merchant's home.

Terborch was also a skilled painter of the genre picture. He was not attracted by the scenes of rustic merriment that delighted so many of the artists of his time, but was more concerned with the elegant surroundings of the wealthy, painted in their own handsome houses. He excelled in depicting silks and satins and draperies, though one critic complains that Terborch could paint "a white satin dress with such brilliance that it jumps right out of the picture" and so destroy the balance of the whole. This is exemplified in *The Satin Gown* in the Dutch royal collection, of which he painted several other versions. Nevertheless, as a painter of a more aristocratic leaning than most artists of his time in Holland, he may have directed the attention of others to the possibilities of depicting scenes other than those of peasant life.

Portrait of Hermanna van der Cruis
London, N. G.

Young Couple Drinking Wine
West Berlin, Staatl. Mus.

The Concert
West Berlin, Staatl. Mus.

113

HENDRICK TERBRUGGHEN

1588-1629

A painter much influenced by Caravaggio

Hendrick Terbrugghen was born in Deventer in 1588. He became a pupil of Abraham Bloemaert before going to Italy in 1604, where he remained until 1614. He then returned to Utrecht, becoming one of the leading members of the Utrecht School. He was a painter of religious subjects and some genre pieces.

Works by Terbrugghen are unknown before 1620, but it is clear that he was the first to bring the ideas of Caravaggio's circle to Utrecht. In his paintings are found elements of Cavaliere d'Arpino in the coloring, of Orazio Gentileschi in the handling of paint, but especially of Caravaggio in some of the figures and in the lighting effects that give volume to the forms. Compared with Joachim Wtewael and Bloemaert, Terbrugghen's art is very silent and still, expressing forms and textures through reflections of light.

Eventually Terbrugghen developed a very personal style. In his coloring and lighting effects he anticipated the great master of the Delft School, Jan Vermeer. Hendrick Terbrugghen died in Utrecht on November 1, 1629.

B. Nicholson   Hendrick Terbrugghen   The Hague, 1958

Fluting Page Boy, 1621
Kassel, Germany, Hessisches Landesmus.

Christ before Pilate, 1620
Copenhagen, Statens Mus.

Fluting Shepherd Boy, 1621
Kassel, Germany, Hessisches Landesmus.

JAN TOOROP

1858-1928

A painter and designer who contributed to the evolution of Symbolism and Art Nouveau

Jan Toorop was born in Purworedjo, Java, in 1858, of parents who were of Dutch-Javanese and British extraction. His early surroundings were to influence his interests and style of painting later in life. Toorop went to Holland in 1869 and there became the pupil of Tetar van Elven. He studied at the Amsterdam Academy from 1880 to 1881, and then at the Brussels Academy until 1885. During this time he was greatly influenced by the work of Jules Bastien-Lepage, Édouard Manet, and James Ensor. Toorop visited England in 1885, and this journey brought him into contact with Pre-Raphaelite painting and also the work of William Blake. The following year he married a girl of English-Scottish parentage.

From 1886 until 1889 Toorop lived partly in London and partly in Brussels. He began to experiment with all the new tendencies in art, and passed from Impressionism to pointillism. His contacts with Ensor and Les XX, and with the poets Émile Verhaeren and Maurice Maeterlinck, brought him into the Symbolist orbit. His conversion to the Roman Catholic faith strengthened his attachment to this movement.

Toorop was a fully developed Symbolist by 1891, and in the following year he produced a series of Symbolist drawings in a linear, rhythmic style. The new English art periodical "The Studio" illustrated some of his work in 1893 and 1894. In his compositions of this date, particularly in drawings such as *The Three Brides*, a parallel to the art of Aubrey Beardsley can be seen. As well as reflecting the influence of William Morris, John Ruskin, and the Pre-Raphaelites, Toorop's work showed the current interest in Oriental and exotic art.

Besides producing paintings, drawings, and prints, Toorop also made designs for furniture, rather in the style of Henri van de Velde. Certainly Toorop had some influence on John Mackintosh and the Glasgow School. He exhibited in Munich in 1893, and with Les XX the following year. He was the most important of the Dutch Symbolist artists. He settled at The Hague, and died there in 1928.

Portrait of the Painter Guillaume Vogels
Brussels, Mus. Royaux des B-A.

HIS WORKS INCLUDE

After the Strike, 1887
Otterlo, Holland, Kröller-Müller
Canal near Middelburg, 1907
The Hague, Gemeentemus.
The Three Brides, 1893
Otterlo, Holland, Kröller-Müller

See also page 252

The Apostles Thomas and Thadeus (detail) 1909
Amsterdam, Stedelijk Mus.

Delftsche Slaolie, 1895
Amsterdam, Stedelijk Mus.

Self-portrait, 1745
The Hague, Mauritshuis

C. Troost

HIS WORKS INCLUDE

Portrait of a Man of Rank, 1723
Amsterdam, Rijksmus.
Three Chiefs of the Surgeons' Guild
1731
Amsterdam, Rijksmus.
Self-portrait, 1737
Amsterdam, Rijksmus.
The Discovery of Jan Claesz, 1738
The Hague, Mauritshuis
Family Group in an Interior, 1739
Amsterdam, Rijksmus.

See also pages 190, 237

CORNELIS TROOST 1697-1750

A typical painter of the 16th century in Holland

Cornelis Troost was born in Amsterdam on October 8, 1697. His paintings consist mainly of portraits of the contemporary *bourgeoisie*, but he also produced conversation pieces, *babbelstukken*, which were scenes of Dutch families in their daily life. These pictures are often humorous and sometimes bear a moral. Other works depict scenes derived from the early 18th-century Dutch theater, especially the comedies of Langendijk, Asselijn, and Alewijn.

Troost also designed scenery for the municipal theater of Amsterdam, and there is a doubtful tradition that he was also an actor there. In some respects he is comparable with William Hogarth and with the Italian Pietro Longhi. In addition to his paintings, Troost also produced many pastels, watercolors, etchings, and mezzotints.

Scene from "Le Malade Imaginaire" by Molière, 1721
East Berlin, Staatl. Mus.

Portrait of a Man of Rank, 1723
Amsterdam, Rijksmus.

W. J v T
()

HIS WORKS INCLUDE

Landscape with Animals
Rotterdam, Boymans-van Beuningen

See also page 191

WOUTER JOHANNES VAN TROOSTWIJK 1782-1810

A painter of landscapes and town views

Wouter Johannes van Troostwijk, born in Amsterdam in 1782, was a pupil of Anthony and Jurriaan Andriessen, and of Anthonie van den Bosch. He also attended the Amsterdam Academy. He painted landscapes and town views in which he demonstrated an independent personal style evolved from Jakob van Ruisdael and Paulus Potter. He died at the early age of 28, having produced only a few works, among them drawings and etchings.

WILLEM VAN DE VELDE the ELDER   1611-1693
WILLEM VAN DE VELDE the YOUNGER   1633-1707
ADRIAEN VAN DE VELDE   1636-1672

WILLEM VAN DE VELDE
the ELDER
Dutch Men-of-War at Sea
Amsterdam, Rijksmus.

A family of accomplished marine and landscape painters

Willem van de Velde the Elder, born in Leiden in 1611, was the younger brother of Jan van de Velde, an able engraver. Willem gained a great reputation as a draftsman of ships and was employed by the Dutch government, at the time of the country's great naval achievements, to make drawings of ships and battles at sea. Many of his drawings are large and executed in black paint and dark ink on a white ground, the contrast being highly effective. Willem was in Amsterdam between 1636 and 1675, and seems sometimes to have sailed with the Dutch fleet. He died in London in 1693, and is buried in St. James's Church, Piccadilly, London, the inscription on his tombstone saying that he painted for Charles II and James II.

Willem van de Velde the Younger followed in the footsteps of his father, with even greater success. He was born in 1633 in Amsterdam and studied under his father. He at first specialized in views of the coast of Holland, and he was one of those artists who made the Scheveningen shore world famous. He attracted the attention and patronage of Charles II of England, who made him court painter in 1674. He died in Greenwich in 1707, leaving behind him many paintings and drawings, now in English collections.

Adriaen van de Velde, Willem the Elder's second son, was born in 1636. He was trained alongside Philips Wouwerman, who apparently taught him much about painting animals. Adriaen was reponsible for the figures and animals in works by Meindert Hobbema, Jakob van Ruisdael, and others, but he was also a fine artist in his own right. He had an eye for a beautiful landscape, with sheep, cows, or goats to enliven it, and his colors are charmingly light. He was delighted by winter scenes, and also painted religious pictures. *The Shore at Scheveningen* is a fine example of his work, and his *Golfers on the Ice near Haarlem*, 1668, is an interesting portrayal of contemporary life.

HIS WORKS INCLUDE
WILLEM VAN DE VELDE
the ELDER
Harbor at Amsterdam, 1686
Amsterdam, Rijksmus.

See also page 237

WILLEM VAN DE VELDE
the YOUNGER
Three Ships in a Gale, 1673
London, N. G.

Admiral Sir L. G. Preston *Sea and River Painters of the Netherlands in the 17th Century* *London, 1937*
N. Maclaren *The Dutch School. N. G. Catalogue* *London, 1960*

HIS WORKS INCLUDE
WILLEM VAN DE VELDE
the YOUNGER
Dutch Men-of-War and Small Vessels
in a Calm, 1657
London, N. G.
Dutch Vessels Close Inshore at
Low Tide, and Men Bathing, 1661
London, N. G.

WILLEM VAN DE VELDE
the YOUNGER
Battle of the Texel (detail) 1673
Greenwich, England, Nat. Maritime Mus.

ADRIAEN VAN DE VELDE
Golfers on the Ice near Haarlem, 1668
London, N. G.

Model for the Tomb of Admiral de
Ruyter, 1676
Amsterdam, Rijksmus.

ROMBOUT VERHULST   1624-1696

A sculptor who brought Italian Baroque ideas to the northern Netherlands

Rombout Verhulst was born in Malines in the southern Netherlands on January
15, 1624, and became one of the principal sculptors of the second half of the 17th
century. He was a pupil of Rombout Verstappen and Frans van Loo. After his
training Verhulst established himself at The Hague. By 1668 he was a member of
the painters' guild there, and in 1676 he became a member of the Confrérie Pictura.
From about 1650 he worked with Artus Quellinus the Elder on the decoration of
the Town Hall in Amsterdam. His style is a blend of vigorous form and exception-
ally delicate treatment of detail. Verhulst is outstanding in his representation of
the human figure. He had learned much from a visit to Italy, and was one of the
sculptors reponsible for bringing the Baroque style to the northern Netherlands.

Verhulst was particularly admired for his sculpture for mausoleums. He also
produced sensitive portraits and was outstanding among contemporary sculptors
for his interpretation of flesh and materials. Hands and heads were particularly
expressively treated. There was little variation in the design of Verhulst's tombs.
Perhaps the most striking are the monuments to Admiral Tromp in Delft and to
Admiral de Ruyter in Amsterdam. In both these works he utilized a large amount
of workshop assistance, but the main figures are by him.

JAN VERMEER 1632-1675

An artist who excelled in the depiction of form and light in Dutch interior scenes

Jan Vermeer was born in 1632 in Delft and died there in 1675. He does not seem to have lived anywhere else or to have traveled. He is now held to have been among the greatest of all Dutch painters, but surprisingly his work aroused no enthusiasm in the art critics of the 18th and early 19th centuries, who ranked him no higher than other painters of his time, such as Pieter de Hooch or Gerard Terborch. This failure to recognize his genius may partly be due to the fact that he painted few pictures and that, of the 40 or so now definitely attributed to him, a number were for a long time thought to be the work of other artists. He rarely signed a picture.

Very little is known of Vermeer's life. He was almost certainly a pupil of Carel Fabritius. He married in 1653 and in that year became a member of the Guild of St. Luke in Delft, of which he was dean for several years. He had 11 children and he seems continually to have needed money. Nevertheless he lived extravagantly, and he died leaving many debts. In 1696, 21 of his pictures were sold by auction in Amsterdam; 19 of them can be identified from the auction catalogue.

Vermeer painted a few portraits and two views of Delft. Apart from these, he began, as did most Dutch painters, by treating Biblical and mythological subjects,

Young Woman Standing by a Virginal, after 1670
London, N. G.

Young Woman Reading a Letter (detail) about 1662
Amsterdam, Rijksmus.

119

and then passed on to portrayals of the Dutch domestic scene. It is with these pictures that he rose to the height of his genius. Even Vermeer's early works are distinguished by a richness of color and adventurousness of treatment that can compare with the work of Rembrandt. These qualities characterized his work throughout his career, and were intensified when he began painting the Dutch interior. He endowed the everyday actions of eating and drinking, letter-writing and music-playing with an enchantment far greater than would seem possible for such mundane pursuits.

Again and again Vermeer used the same pieces of furniture and decorations accompanying the same women. An earthenware jug appears more than once, similarly a chair with a high back, carvings of small lions, and a carpet draped over a table. His use of mirrors has intrigued many students of his pictures. It is sometimes difficult to determine whether he was painting a scene directly or the

The Little Street, about 1658
Amsterdam, Rijksmus.

The Procuress, 1656
Dresden, Gemäldegal.

A Young Woman Seated
at a Virginal, about 1670
London, N. G.

reflection as it appeared to him in a mirror.

Vermeer was a master of light and shade. In his interiors the light streams in, predominantly from left to right, and the marble floors and white walls help to enhance its radiance. Both figures and furniture are painted with the utmost minuteness, so that the whole effect is a precise and detailed record of the way men and women lived, of the clothes they wore, and of the houses they occupied, in the Delft of his day. Vermeer's understanding of color and his delight in the contrast between the simplicity of some of his models and the comparative grandeur of their surroundings, mark him as an artist of the highest order.

J. Leymarie   Dutch Painting from Geertgen tot Sint Jans to Vermeer   Lausanne, 1956
N. Maclaren   The Dutch School, N. G. Catalogue   London, 1960
J. Dupont and F. Matthey   Caravaggio to Vermeer   Skira, New York, 1961

The Geographer, 1669
Frankfurt-am-Main, Städelsches Kunstinst.

Young Woman with a Water Jug, 1660
New York, Met. Mus., Gift of
Henry G. Marquand, 1889

Girl with a Pearl,
about 1660
The Hague, Mauritshuis

121

FLORIS VERSTER

1861-1927

Self-portrait, 1921
Rotterdam, Boymans-van Beuningen

HIS WORKS INCLUDE

The Dead Swan, 1886
Rotterdam, Boymans-van Beuningen
Landscape
Otterlo, Holland, Kröller-Müller
Flowers
Amsterdam, Rijksmus.

See also page 204

A painter who furthered the spread of coloristic and intimate realism

The work of Floris Verster, who was born in Leiden in 1861, consists mostly of still-lifes, town views, and a few portraits. Influenced at first by George Hendrik Breitner and Jan Hendrik Weissenbruch, he achieved, especially after 1890, a personal interpretation of Impressionism without repeating what had been done before him.

Verster's crayon drawings, and later his paintings, show a renewed mastery of form. At the same time his colors and touch developed from a passionate vividness into an intense stillness. His still-lifes may be compared with those of 17th-century Dutch artists such as Pieter Claesz.

Verster was of great importance to the spread of realism in Holland. In his later years he regained his sensitive visual objectivity. He was in touch with the literary revival in Holland in the 1880's, and was the friend of the poet Albert Verwey.

MICHEL VERVOORT

1667-1737

A sculptor in both the Baroque and classical styles

Michel Vervoort was born in Antwerp on January 3, 1667. He became a pupil of Henri Cosyns, and by 1690 was a member of the guild in Antwerp. About this date he worked with Gaspar Pieter Verbruggen the Younger on the carving, *The Hill of Calvary*, for the Dominican church in Antwerp. Soon after this Vervoort went to Italy, staying about 10 or 14 years in Rome. It is probable that he later went to France and also to London. He eventually returned to Antwerp in 1704.

Vervoort did a great deal of work for churches in Antwerp. For Antwerp Cathedral he carved a pulpit with rich ornamentation and statues representing the four quarters of the world. He also collaborated with Artus Quellinus the Younger on two carved confessionals for the Church of St. Jacques, and later on a group, *The Flagellation*, for an altar. In 1719 his monument to the Le Candèle family, with a bas-relief, *The Raising of Lazarus*, was erected. Vervoort carved an elaborate confessional for the Jesuit church of St. Charles Borromeo, which had medallions illustrating the lives of Ignazius Loyala and Francis Xavier. He executed the confessional with the help of Jan Pieter van Baurscheit the Elder.

The most elaborate piece of sculpture by Vervoort is the pulpit in Malines

HIS WORKS INCLUDE

Monument to Bishop de Precipiano
1709
Malines, Cath.
Lectern, with statue of the
Archangel Michael, 1725
Ghent, St. Michel
Congressional, with bas-relief of the
Good Shepherd, 1726
Ghent, St. Michel

See also page 276

Cathedral, which is even more exuberant than Gianlorenzo Bernini's fountain in the Piazza Navona in Rome. In a rock built up of pieces of wood, he hollowed a cave in which is depicted a dramatic conversion of St. Norbert. This work was executed in 1721. In the transept of the Jesuit church in Malines Vervoort later set up his bas-relief *The Raising of the Crosses*. He died in Antwerp in 1737, after a long and successful career.

H. Gerson and E. H. ter Kuile   Art and Architecture in Belgium 1600-1800   London, 1960

PAUL DE VIGNE   1843-1901

A sculptor in the Neoclassical style of the 19th century

Paul de Vigne was born in Ghent on April 26, 1843, the son of a sculptor. He became a student at the Ghent Academy, under Jan Robert Calloigne, and later he studied at Antwerp and Louvain. De Vigne won the Prix de Rome in 1869. He traveled to Italy and stayed in Florence and Rome. In 1872 he returned to Ghent for some time, but during the 1880's he was in Paris. It was here in 1884 that he made his statue *Immortality*. On his return to Belgium, de Vigne spent most of his time in Brussels. He suffered a nervous breakdown in 1896, and had to stay for some time in a clinic in Evere, where he died in 1901.

In the years preceding his nervous disorder de Vigne produced several monumental works. In 1887 he made the monument to Breydel and de Coninck in the Great Market Place of Bruges. He sculpted a group, *Triumph of Art*, for the façade of the Musées Royaux des Beaux-Arts in Brussels. In 1897 a monument, on which he collaborated with Julien Dillens and others, was unveiled in Anspach. For this work de Vigne had sculpted the crowned statue of St. Michael, and designed the reliefs on the pedestal.

De Vigne's style was eclectic. The predominant inspiration came from Parisian sculptors, but the influence of Neoclassicism was evident before he adopted the realistic style of Jean Baptiste Carpeaux. Paul de Vigne had no particular influence on contemporary Belgian sculptors.

Immortality, 1884
Brussels, Mus. Royaux des B-A.

HIS WORKS INCLUDE
Portrait of Marnix van St. Aldegonde
Antwerp, Mus. Royal des B-A.
Italian Woman
Brussels, Mus. Royaux des B-A.

See also page 280

ADRIAEN DE VRIES   about 1550-1626

A portraitist, sculptor, and carver

The dates in the documentary evidence of Adriaen de Vries's life are confusing, since there appears to have been another artist of the same name who entered the Antwerp guild in 1634, and died in 1650. Adriaen de Vries, however, was born at The Hague about 1550. He became a pupil of Giovanni da Bologna in Florence. In 1588 he entered the service of the duke of Savoy, Charles Emmanuel, in Turin, and in 1593, with Rome as his base, he worked for Emperor Rudolph II in Prague.

De Vries also visited Augsburg, where in 1596 he took over the execution of the

HIS WORKS INCLUDE
Hercules, about 1585
Rotterdam, Boymans-van Beuningen
Portrait of a Man
Dresden, Gemäldegal.

See also page 267

Mercury Fountain (detail)
about 1596-1602
Augsburg

Mercury Fountain which he finished in 1599 or 1602. In 1601, probably due to help from Bartholomeus Spranger, he was appointed court sculptor to the emperor, and from that time he lived in Prague. He was active there until the death of the emperor in 1612. He then carried out various monuments for European royalty. In 1617 he made a fountain for the castle of Frederiksborg for Christian IV of Denmark. For the prince of Schaumburg-Lippe, de Vries constructed a mausoleum, on which he worked from 1618 to 1620, and about 1620 he made a fountain for the ducal palace in Prague. He died in that city in 1626.

HIS WORKS INCLUDE

The Death of the Virgin
Amsterdam, Rijksmus.
Altar of the Confraternity of
Our Lady, 1475-77
's Hertogenbosch, Cath.

See also page 260

ADRIAEN VAN WESEL   about 1420 - about 1500

A sculptor of religious subjects characteristic of the 15th century

Some years ago P. T. A. Swillens identified the Master of the Music-making Angels and the Master of the Death of The Virgin with Adriaen van Wesel. These names were derived from wood sculptures of these subjects in the Rijksmuseum, Amsterdam.

Van Wesel lived in Utrecht in the 15th century and is often mentioned in the Utrecht archives. Most of his works are executed in a technique that is a combination of relief and free-standing sculpture. This approach to form is also reflected in contemporary painting. He also made sculptures in stone; for example, those in the chapel of Rudolf van Diepenholt in Utrecht Cathedral. In 1475-77 he executed an altar for 's Hertogenbosch Cathedral in collaboration with the painter Hieronymus Bosch. Adriaen van Wesel died about 1500.

HIS WORKS INCLUDE

The Deposition, about 1438
Madrid, Prado
The Nativity, about 1438
Granada, Royal Chapel
Pietà, about 1438
Granada, Royal Chapel
The Baptism of Christ, about 1450
West Berlin, Staatl. Mus.
The Madonna and Child, about 1450
Frankfurt-am-Main, Städelsches Kunstinst.

See also pages 133, 211

ROGER VAN DER WEYDEN   1399/1400-1464

A major artist of the mid-15th century in Flanders

Roger van der Weyden, or Rogier de la Pasture, was born in Tournai in 1399/1400. He was apprenticed to Robert Campin, believed to be the Master of Flémalle, at the relatively late age of 27 or 28. It is usually presumed that previously he had attained a mastership in some other craft, perhaps that of goldsmith. About 1426 he married a woman from Brussels, and when he had completed his apprenticeship he moved to Brussels and there became the city painter in 1435.

The Holy Year of 1450 attracted pilgrims to Italy from all over Europe, and among them was van der Weyden. It is not known whether he reached Rome, but he certainly visited Florence and a number of other towns in northern Italy. His work at this time shows a marked affinity to his Florentine contemporaries, particularly to Fra Angelico and Gentile da Fabriano. Two paintings believed to have been painted either in Italy, or shortly after his visit there, are *The Entombment* and *The Madonna and Four Saints*. Both may have been commissioned by the Medici family as they bear its arms.

Technically van der Weyden achieved as great a perfection as the van Eycks, though stylistically he was closer, especially in facial types, to his teacher Campin. His rich, subtle tone and color help to create an intensely spiritual atmosphere that distinguishes his work. His portraits, of which there are a number, possess a psychological depth quite new in Flemish painting. These are sometimes found in a diptych, Madonna and Child, Christ, or a saint, on one wing, and the portrait of the donor on the other. These diptych portraits became very popular and set a fashion continued by Hans Memling and Dieric Bouts.

Van der Weyden died in Brussels in 1464. Of his four surviving children, two became painters and one a goldsmith.

J. A. Crowe and G. B. Calvalcaselle   Early Flemish Painters   London, 1879
E. G. Troche   Painting in the Netherlands in the 15th and 16th Centuries   London, 1936
W. Vogelsang   Form and Color: Roger van der Weyden's Pietà   New York, 1949

Portrait of Charles the Bold
East Berlin, Staatl. Mus.

Christ the Redeemer between The Virgin and St. John the Evangelist
Paris, Louvre

Francesco d'Este (about 1430-after 1447)
New York, Met. Mus., Michael Friedsam Coll., 1931

Head of Dr. C. A. Lion Cachet, 1931
Otterlo, Holland, Kröller-Müller

HIS WORKS INCLUDE

Farmer with a Scythe
Otterlo, Holland, Kröller-Müller

Three Chickens, 1895
Otterlo, Holland, Kröller-Müller

Little Boy, 1900
Otterlo, Holland, Kröller-Müller

See also pages 284, 285

LAMBERTUS ZIJL   1866-1947

A sculptor and medalist

Born in Rotterdam in 1866, Lambertus Zijl studied at the Quellinus School of Sculpture and afterwards at the Amsterdam School of Applied Arts. There he met Joseph Mendes da Costa, with whom he founded the anti-academic society, Labor et Ars. In 1887 he made one of his first medals for this society.

After a short period of collaboration with the more complex da Costa, Zijl was employed in a workshop of applied arts in Amsterdam. He met the architect Hendrik Petrus Berlage, and began to make stylized sculptures for his buildings, aiming to blend them with Berlage's architecture. He worked with other architects as well, notably with Kropholler on churches and town halls, and with Gustave Staal and de Bazel. He also collaborated with the interior decorator Lion Cachet on various commissions between 1907 and 1928.

In addition to his architectural sculpture, Zijl also produced portraits and small bronze figures. Like da Costa, he found his subjects for these figures in the daily life of the streets and markets of Amsterdam. In contrast to his formalized architectural works, his style in these was impressionistic, executed with a free modeling technique. With da Costa, Zijl stood at the beginning of a revival in Dutch sculpture. He died in 1947.

Youth
Otterlo, Holland, Kröller-Müller

The Sea, 1915 (bronze relief)
Otterlo, Holland, Kröller-Müller

Color Plates

MASTER OF FLÉMALLE sometimes identified with ROBERT CAMPIN The Annunciation: central panel from the
Mérode Altarpiece, 1425-28 *oil on panel 25¼ × 24⅞ in.*
New York, Metropolitan Museum of Art, Cloisters Collection

MELCHIOR BROEDERLAM The Presentation in the Temple and the Flight into Egypt
(detail) 1394-99 *oil on panel* 65¾ × 49¼ *in.*
Dijon, Musée des Beaux-Arts

JAN VAN EYCK The Adoration of the Holy Lamb: center panel from the Ghent Altarpiece, 1432 *oil on panel 53×93 in.*
Ghent, Cathedral of St. Bavon

JAN VAN EYCK Portrait of Giovanni Arnolfini and his Wife, 1434 *oil on panel 32¼ × 23¼ in.*
London, National Gallery

JAN VAN EYCK   The Madonna of Canon van der Paele, 1436   *oil on panel   48×62 in.*
Bruges, Musée Communal

PETRUS CHRISTUS Portrait of a Lady of the Talbot Family, about 1446 *oil on panel* *11 × 8¼ in.*
West Berlin, Staatliche Museen

ROGER VAN DER WEYDEN The Last Judgment (center panels) about 1450 *tempera* *86 × 214½ in.*
Beaune, l'Hôtel-Dieu

133

DIERIC BOUTS The Last Supper, about 1467 *oil on panel* *114 × 71 in.*
Louvain, Belgium, St. Pierre

HUGO VAN DER GOES The Adoration of the Shepherds: central panel from the Portinari Altarpiece, about 1476
oil on panel 99⅜ × 119⅝ in.
Florence, Uffizi

HANS MEMLING The Adoration of the Magi, 1479   *oil on panel* $18\frac{7}{8} \times 22\frac{1}{4}$ *in.*
Bruges, Hospital of St. John

HANS MEMLING Portrait of Martin van Nieuwenhove, 1487   *oil on panel $17\frac{3}{8} \times 13$ in.*
Bruges, Hospital of St. John

JOOS VAN GHENT The Institution of the Eucharist, about 1474 *oil on panel* $113 \times 122\frac{7}{8}$ *in.*
Urbino, Italy, Ducal Palace, Gallery of the Marches

138

GERARD DAVID The Madonna of the Milk Soup, about 1520 *oil on panel 14 × 11½ in.*
Brussels, Musées Royaux des Beaux-Arts

GEERTGEN TOT SINT JANS St. John the Baptist in the Wilderness, middle period
oil on panel   16¼ × 11 in.
West Berlin, Staatliche Museen

HIERONYMUS BOSCH   The Ship of Fools, after 1500
oil on panel   22 × 12 in.
Paris, Louvre

QUENTIN MASSYS The Moneylender and his Wife, 1514 *oil on panel* *28 × 27 in.*
Paris, Louvre

JAN GOSSAERT called MABUSE   Portrait of Baudouin of Burgundy   *oil on panel   21¼ × 15⅜ in.*
West Berlin, Staatliche Museen

JOOS VAN CLEVE Portrait of Eleanora of Hapsburg, about 1530   *oil on panel*   *14 × 11¼ in.*
Vienna, Kunsthistorisches Museum

JAN VAN SCOREL Portrait of a Young Scholar, 1531   *oil on panel   14×14 in.*
Rotterdam, Museum Boymans-van Beuningen

PIETER BRUEGEL the ELDER   Landscape with the Fall of Icarus, about 1563   *oil on panel   29 × 44⅛ in.*
Brussels, Musées Royaux des Beaux-Arts

PIETER BRUEGEL the ELDER   Hunters in the Snow, 1565   *oil on panel*   *46 × 63¾ in.*
Vienna, Kunsthistorisches Museum

PIETER BRUEGEL the ELDER   The Peasant Wedding (detail) about 1568   *oil on panel* $44\frac{3}{4} \times 64\frac{1}{4}$ *in.*
Vienna, Kunsthistorisches Museum

PIETER BRUEGEL the ELDER The Parable of the Blind Leading the Blind, 1568 *tempera on canvas* *34×60½ in.*
Naples, Galleria Nazionale

HENDRICK AVERCAMP Winter Landscape *oil on panel · $30\frac{1}{4} \times 52$ in.*
Amsterdam, Rijksmuseum

PIETER AERTSEN The Egg Dance, 1557 *oil on panel 33 × 50 in.*
Amsterdam, Rijksmuseum

SIR ANTHONIS MOR Portrait of a Goldsmith, 1564 *oil on panel* $46\frac{1}{4} \times 33\frac{3}{8}$ *in.*
The Hague, Mauritshuis

SIR PETER PAUL RUBENS   The Artist and his First Wife, Isabella Brandt, in the Honeysuckle
Bower, 1609   *oil on canvas   70 × 53 in.*
Munich, Alte Pinakothek

SIR PETER PAUL RUBENS The Adoration of the Magi, 1624 *oil on canvas 176×72½ in.*
Antwerp, Musée Royal des Beaux-Arts

SIR PETER PAUL RUBENS The Straw Hat, about 1626 *oil on canvas 31 × 21¼ in.*
London, National Gallery

SIR PETER PAUL RUBENS Landscape with Rainbow, about 1640 *oil on panel* *37 × 48⅜ in.*
Munich, Alte Pinakothek

SIR PETER PAUL RUBENS   Helena Fourment and her Children, about 1635
oil on canvas $44\frac{1}{2} \times 72\frac{1}{2}$ *in.*
Paris, Louvre

JACOB JORDAENS The King Drinks, 1638 *oil on canvas 61¾ × 82⅝ in.*
Brussels, Musées Royaux des Beaux-Arts

SIR ANTHONY VAN DYCK   Portrait of the Painter Cornelis de Wael, about 1627
oil on canvas   103½ × 64⅝ in.
Antwerp, Musée Royal des Beaux-Arts

FRANS HALS The Merry Drinker, 1627 *oil on canvas* *32 × 26 in.*
Amsterdam, Rijksmuseum

FRANS HALS The Lady Governors of the Old Men's Home at Haarlem, 1664   *oil on canvas*   *66⅞×98 in.*
Haarlem, Frans Hals Museum

BALTHASAR VAN DER AST Flowers and Fruit, 1620 *oil on panel* *19¼ × 27⅝ in.*
Amsterdam, Rijksmuseum

HENDRICK TERBRUGGHEN Jacob Reproaching Laban, 1627 *oil on canvas* $38\frac{1}{2} \times 45$ *in.*
London, National Gallery

HERCULES SEGHERS Landscape *oil on canvas $21\frac{3}{8} \times 39\frac{3}{8}$ in.*
Florence, Uffizi

REMBRANDT VAN RYN Landscape with a Stone Bridge, about 1638 *oil on panel* $11\frac{1}{2} \times 17\frac{1}{2}$ *in.*
Amsterdam, Rijksmuseum

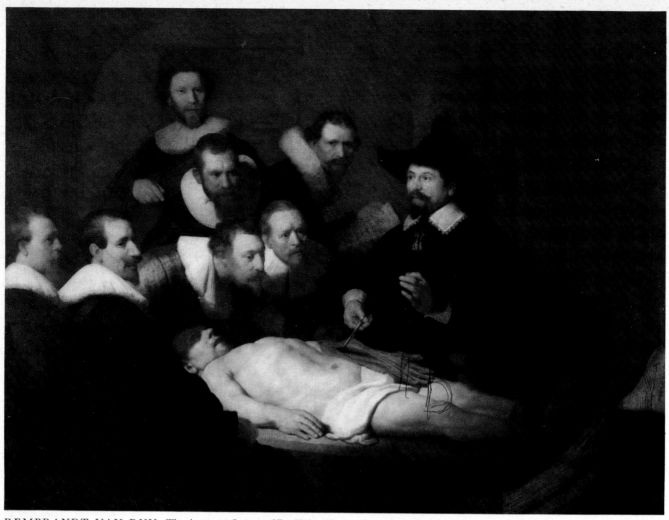

REMBRANDT VAN RYN   The Anatomy Lesson of Dr. Tulp, 1632   *oil on canvas*   *64 × 85 in.*
The Hague, Mauritshuis

REMBRANDT VAN RYN Portrait of Titus, about 1656 *oil on canvas* $52\frac{3}{8} \times 40\frac{7}{8}$ *in.*
Vienna, Kunsthistorisches Museum

REMBRANDT VAN RYN The Flagellation, 1658 *oil on canvas* $36\frac{1}{8} \times 28\frac{3}{8}$ *in.*
Darmstadt, Hessisches Landesmuseums

REMBRANDT VAN RYN Self-portrait, 1658 *oil on canvas 52⅝×40⅞ in.*
New York, Frick Collection

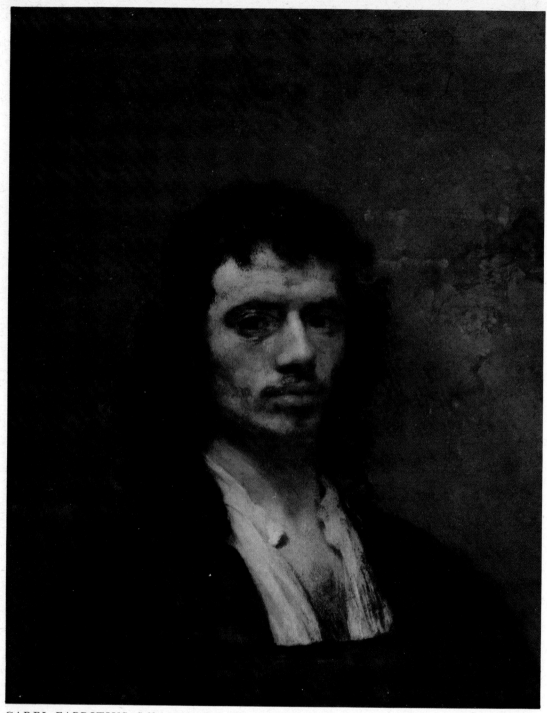

CAREL FABRITIUS Self-portrait, 1646   *oil on panel* $25\frac{1}{2} \times 19$ *in.*
Rotterdam, Museum Boymans-van Beuningen

NICOLAS MAES   Woman Spinning, 1655   *oil on panel   16¼ × 13 in.*
Amsterdam, Rijksmuseum

GERARD TERBORCH   Paternal Advice, about 1655   *oil on canvas*   *28 × 28¾ in.*
Amsterdam, Rijksmuseum

JAN STEEN The Artist's Family *oil on canvas* $53\frac{7}{8} \times 64\frac{1}{4}$ *in.*
The Hague, Mauritshuis

ADRIAEN BROUWER The Operation *oil on panel* $12\frac{1}{4} \times 15\frac{3}{4}$ *in.*
Munich, Alte Pinakothek

ADRIAEN VAN OSTADE   The Peasants' Party, about 1659   *oil on panel   18¼ × 25 in.*
The Hague, Mauritshuis

PIETER DE HOOCH   Interior of a Tavern, 1658   *oil on canvas   30 × 26 in.*
London, Royal Collection

176

JAN VERMEER Maid Pouring Milk, 1658 *oil on canvas* $17\frac{3}{4} \times 16\frac{1}{8}$ *in.*
Amsterdam, Rijksmuseum

JAN VERMEER   View of Delft, 1658   *oil on canvas   39 × 46⅛ in.*
The Hague, Mauritshuis

JAN VERMEER The Artist's Studio, 1665 *oil on canvas* *47 × 39¼ in.*
Vienna, Kunsthistorisches Museum

PIETER SAENREDAM   Interior of the Buurkerk at Utrecht, 1644   *oil on panel   23¼ × 20 in.*
London, National Gallery

PIETER CLAESZ Still-life with Wine Glass, 1642 *oil on panel* *27⅛ × 20⅞ in.*
Rotterdam, Museum Boymans-van Beuningen

JAN FYT Hounds Resting *oil on panel* 41⅜×69¼ *in.*
Antwerp, Musée Royal des Beaux-Arts

ABRAHAM HENDRICKZ VAN BEYEREN Still-life with Fruit *oil on panel* *17¾ × 24¾ in.*
Munich, Alte Pinakothek

JAN VAN GOYEN   River Scene, 1655   *oil on panel   16¼ × 22 in.*
The Hague, Mauritshuis

AERT VAN DER NEER Moonlit Landscape *oil on panel* $6\frac{7}{8} \times 15$ *in.*
West Berlin, Staatliche Museen

PHILIPS DE KONINCK   View of the River Waal, 1654   *oil on canvas   59 × 79⅞ in.*
Copenhagen, Statens Museum for Kunst

JAKOB VAN RUISDAEL The Waterfall, about 1670 *oil on canvas* $55\frac{7}{8} \times 76\frac{3}{4}$ *in.*
Amsterdam, Rijksmuseum

MEINDERT HOBBEMA   The Avenue at Middelharnis, 1689   *oil on canvas* $40\frac{3}{4} \times 55\frac{1}{2}$ *in.*
London, National Gallery

JAN JOSEF HOREMANS the ELDER   Garden with Figures on a Terrace, 1735   *oil on canvas* $25\frac{3}{4} \times 31\frac{1}{4}$ *in.*
London, collection Rex A. L. Cohen

CORNELIS TROOST   The Wedding of Kloris and Roosje, about 1739   *pastel on paper   25¼ × 32⅜ in.*
The Hague, Mauritshuis

WOUTER JOHANNES VAN TROOSTWIJK   The Raampoortje Gate at Amsterdam, 1809
oil on canvas   22¼ × 18⅞ in.
Amsterdam, Rijksmuseum

FRANÇOIS JOSEPH NAVEZ Self-portrait, 1826 *oil on canvas*
Brussels, Musées Royaux des Beaux-Arts

HENDRIK LEYS The Bird Catcher, 1866 *oil on panel 24 × 36¼ in.*
Antwerp, Musée Royal des Beaux-Arts

ALFRED STEVENS   The Desperate Woman   *oil on panel*   *40⅛ × 28 in.*
Antwerp, Musée Royal des Beaux-Arts

HENRI DE BRAEKELEER Man in a Chair, 1875 *oil on canvas* $31\frac{1}{8} \times 24\frac{3}{4}$ *in.*
Antwerp, Musée Royal des Beaux-Arts

JAKOB MARIS The Schreijerstoren at Amsterdam *oil on canvas $27\frac{1}{2} \times 58\frac{1}{4}$ in.*
The Hague, Gemeentemuseum, acquired with the support of the "Vereeniging Rembrandt."

MATTHIJS MARIS Memory of Amsterdam, 1871 *oil on canvas* $18\frac{1}{4} \times 11\frac{3}{4}$ *in.*
Amsterdam, Rijksmuseum

JOHAN BARTHOLD JONGKIND Demolition of the Rue des Francs, 1868 *oil on canvas* 13¾ × 16½ *in.*
The Hague, Gemeentemuseum

ISAAC ISRAELS   Café Chantant, about 1895   *oil on canvas* $35\frac{1}{2} \times 41\frac{1}{4}$ *in.*
Otterlo, Holland, Rijksmuseum Kröller-Müller

FÉLICIEN ROPS Death at the Ball, 1893 *oil on canvas* $59\frac{1}{2} \times 33\frac{1}{2}$ *in.*
Otterlo, Holland, Rijksmuseum Kröller-Müller

JAMES ENSOR People in Masks Fighting over a Hanged Man, 1891 *oil on canvas 23¼ × 29⅛ in.*
Antwerp, Musée Royal des Beaux-Arts

VINCENT VAN GOGH The Olive Grove, 1889 *oil on canvas* $27\frac{3}{4} \times 35\frac{1}{2}$ *in.*
Otterlo, Holland, Rijksmuseum Kröller-Müller

VINCENT VAN GOGH Self-portrait, Saint-Rémy, 1890 *oil on canvas 25⅝ × 21¼ in.*
Paris, Musée de l'Impressionnisme, gift of Paul and Marguerite Gachet

FLORIS VERSTER Still-life with Bottles, 1892 *oil on canvas* $37\frac{3}{8} \times 26\frac{3}{8}$ in.
Otterlo, Holland, Rijksmuseum Kröller-Müller

GEORGE-HENDRIK BREITNER Amsterdam; The Dam at Night, 1893 *oil on canvas* 57⅞ × 87¾ *in.*
Amsterdam, Stedelijk Museum

JACOB SMITS Evening Landscape, between 1901-14 *oil on canvas 37 × 39⅜ in.*
Antwerp, Musée Royal des Beaux-Arts

Drawings

JAN VAN EYCK Portrait of Cardinal Albergati, 1431
silverpoint on white paper $8\frac{1}{4} \times 7\frac{1}{4}$ in.
Dresden, Gemäldegalerie

JAN VAN EYCK St. Barbara, 1437
silverpoint on wood $12\frac{1}{4} \times 7\frac{1}{4}$ *in.*
Antwerp, Musée Royal des Beaux-Arts

HUGO VAN DER GOES Jacob and Rachel, about 1470-75
bistre, pen, and wash heightened with white on gray paper   12 × 22 in.
Oxford, England, Christ Church College

ROGER VAN DER WEYDEN
St. Mary Magdalen, about 1452
silverpoint on cream-colored paper   7 × 5¼ in.
London, British Museum

DIERIC BOUTS   Portrait of a Man, about 1462   *silverpoint on white paper*   *5¼ × 4¼ in.*
Northampton, Mass., Smith College

HIERONYMUS BOSCH
Study for The Ship of Fools,
after 1500   *brush and wash heightened*
with white on gray paper   *10 × 6¼ in.*
Paris, Louvre

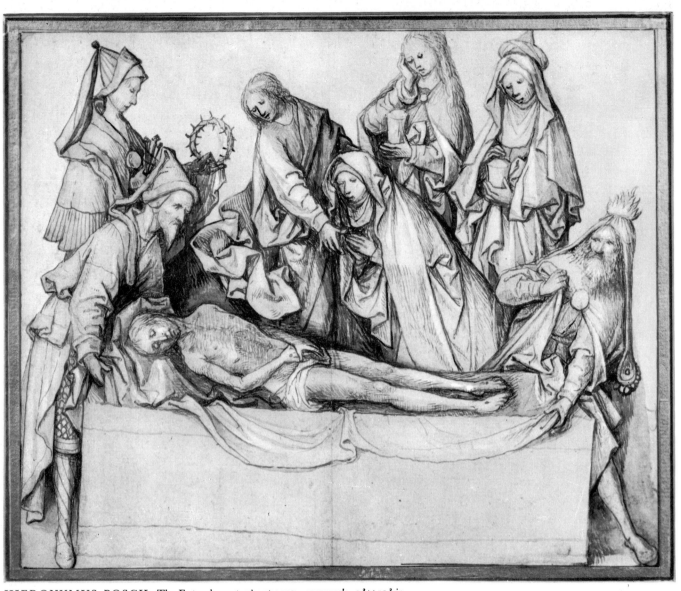

HIERONYMUS BOSCH   The Entombment, about 1507   *gray wash* $9\frac{3}{4} \times 13\frac{3}{4}$ in.
London, British Museum

HIERONYMUS BOSCH The Man-Tree *pen* $10\frac{3}{4} \times 8\frac{1}{4}$ *in.*
Vienna, Albertina

LUCAS VAN LEYDEN Girl Reading, 1522
black chalk $11\frac{3}{4} \times 7\frac{1}{2}$ *in.*
Vienna, Albertina

LUCAS VAN LEYDEN Portrait of a Man, about 1518 *black chalk 13 × 13 in.*
Paris, Louvre

PIETER BRUEGEL the ELDER
Big Fishes Eat Little Fishes, 1556
pen and bistre $8\frac{1}{2} \times 11\frac{3}{4}$ *in.*
Vienna, Albertina

PIETER BRUEGEL the ELDER
The Painter and the Connoisseur, about 1565
pen and bistre $10 \times 8\frac{1}{2}$ *in.*
Vienna, Albertina

PIETER BRUEGEL the ELDER
Standing Peasant, about 1564-66   *pen and crayon* $7\frac{1}{2} \times 4\frac{3}{4}$ *in.*
Rotterdam, Museum Boymans-van Beuningen

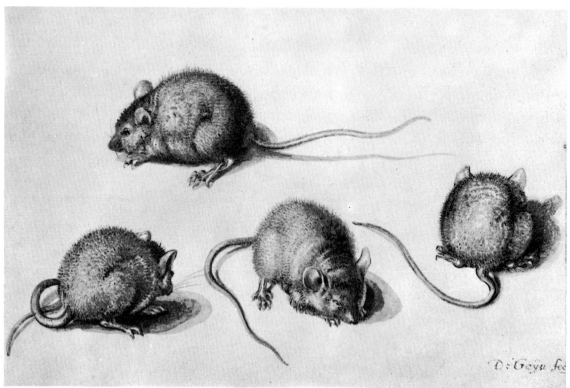

JAKOB DE GHEYN I   Studies of Mice
pen and wash on prepared ground $5 \times 7\frac{1}{4}$ *in.*   *Amsterdam, Rijksmuseum*

BARTHOLOMEUS SPRANGER
St. Martin
*pen and wash heightened with body color
on gray paper   9¼ × 4¾ in.
Amsterdam, Rijksmuseum*

HENDRIK GOLTZIUS   Portrait of Giovanni da Bologna, 1591   *chalk* $14\frac{3}{4} \times 11\frac{3}{4}$ *in.*
Haarlem, Teyler's Museum

JOOS DE MOMPER
Winter Landscape, about 1600-1610
pen with brown ink   10¼ × 16¾ in.
Cambridge, England, Fitzwilliam Museum

Attributed to PIETER BRUEGEL the YOUNGER
Praying Shepherd   *pen and bistre   11½ × 7¾ in.*
Budapest, Museum of Fine Arts

JAKOB DE GHEYN II
Death and the Woman, 1600   *pen* $6\frac{3}{4} \times 5\frac{1}{4}$ *in.*
Amsterdam, Rijksmuseum

JAN BRUEGEL the **ELDER**   River with Wooden Bridge
pen and wash $6\frac{1}{4} \times 4$ *in.*
Paris, Louvre

222

SIR PETER PAUL RUBENS The Duke of Lerma, 1603
black chalk, pen, and bistre $11\frac{3}{4} \times 8\frac{1}{4}$ in.
Paris, Louvre

ROELANT SAVERY Seated Monkey *colored chalk* $16 \times 11\frac{3}{4}$ in.
Amsterdam, Rijksmuseum

SIR PETER PAUL RUBENS Landscape, about 1630 *black chalk with red and white highlights* *15 × 19¼ in.*
Oxford, England, Ashmolean

SIR PETER PAUL RUBENS
Portrait of a Young Woman, about 1628-35
black chalk with sanguine and white highlights   18¾ × 13¾ in.
Rotterdam, Museum Boymans-van Beuningen

SIR PETER PAUL RUBENS
Portrait of Isabella Brandt, about 1625
black, red, and white chalk   15 × 11½ in.
London, British Museum

SIR PETER PAUL RUBENS Self-portrait, about 1640
black chalk heightened with white 18 × 11¼ in.
Paris, Louvre

Attributed to FRANS HALS
Standing Cavalier *chalk 16¾ × 9 in.*
Amsterdam, Rijksmuseum

JACOB JORDAENS   The Deposition, about 1650
black chalk with gray wash   8¼ × 8¼ in.
Paris, collection F. Lugt, Institut Néerlandais

JACOB JORDAENS   Old Man with a Wine Glass, about 1640
red and black chalk heightened with white   7½ × 5½ in.
Cambridge, England, Fitzwilliam Museum

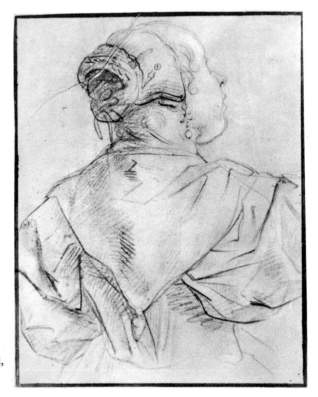

JACOB JORDAENS   Young Woman Seen from Behind,
about 1652   *black and red chalk   8¾ × 6¾ in.*
West Berlin, Staatliche Museen

SIR ANTHONY VAN DYCK St. Mary's Church at Rye, England
1634 *pen and bistre* 6¼ × 10¾ *in.*
Florence, Uffizi

SIR ANTHONY VAN DYCK Study for St. Sebastian,
about 1620 *black chalk heightened with white on blue paper* 20¾ × 16¼ *in.*
Paris, collection F. Lugt, Institut Néerlandais

SIR ANTHONY VAN DYCK   Portrait of Pieter Bruegel the Younger   *pen   10½ × 7¼ in.*
Haarlem, Teyler's Museum

PIETER SAENREDAM   The Square at Haarlem, 1629   *pen and wash*   5×7¼ *in.*
The Hague, Koninklijke Bibliotheek

REMBRANDT VAN RYN Lioness Devouring a Bird, 1641
chalk and wash   5 × 9¼ in.
London, British Museum

REMBRANDT VAN RYN Saskia with a Child, about 1636
pen and wash   7¼ × 5¼ in.
New York, Pierpont Morgan Library

REMBRANDT VAN RYN Two Farms, 1650-58
pen and wash $7\frac{3}{4} \times 12\frac{1}{4}$ in.
West Berlin, Staatliche Museen

REMBRANDT VAN RYN
Hendrickje Stoffels Sleeping, about 1660-69
wash drawing $9\frac{3}{4} \times 7\frac{3}{4}$ in.
London, British Museum

232

REMBRANDT VAN RYN Portrait of Jan Six *silverpoint* $9\frac{1}{4} \times 7\frac{3}{4}$ *in.*
Amsterdam, Jan Six Foundation

CORNELIUS SAFTLEVEN Bear, 1649 *colored chalk and wash*
7¾ × 11¼ in.
Amsterdam, Rijksmuseum

ADRIAEN VAN OSTADE Peasant Family,
about 1640-50 *pen, wash, and bistre 9½ × 7¾ in.*
Budapest, Museum of Fine Arts

GERARD DOU Man Trimming His Quill
chalk 11¼ × 7¼ in.
Amsterdam, Museum Fodor

NICOLAS MAES Girl Selling Oranges
chalk 8×5¼ in.
Chantilly, Musée Condé

AELBERT CUYP Man on a Horse,
about 1650-60 *black chalk and wash 8×4¾ in.*
Cambridge, England, Fitzwilliam Museum

JAN VAN GOYEN Winter Games near Leiden, 1653
black chalk and wash 4¾×8 in.
Amsterdam, Rijksmuseum

PAULUS POTTER   Stags in the Forest   *chalk   9½ × 12½ in.*
Amsterdam, Rijksmuseum

JAKOB VAN RUISDAEL   The Jewish Cemetery   *black chalk with wash*
Haarlem, Teyler's Museum

CORNELIS TROOST Portrait of a Young Girl
pastel 15 × 11 in.
Amsterdam, Museum Fodor

WILLEM VAN DE VELDE the ELDER Ship
pen and wash 9½ × 7¾ in.
East Berlin, Staatliche Museen

JOHANNES BOSBOOM
Interior of the Nieuwe Kerk in Amsterdam, 1844
black chalk and wash   *16 × 11¾ in.*
Otterlo, Holland, Rijksmuseum Kröller-Müller

238

JOHAN BARTHOLD JONGKIND
Lesdiguières Bridge near Grenoble, 1883 *wash drawing* $11\frac{1}{2} \times 19\frac{1}{2}$ *in.*
Paris, Louvre

HENRI DE BRAEKELEER The Little Gate
crayon $6\frac{1}{4} \times 4\frac{3}{4}$ *in.*
Brussels, Bibliothèque Royale

MATTHIJS MARIS
Young Girl Sewing
black chalk   27 × 15¾ in.
The Hague, Gemeentemuseum

FÉLICIEN ROPS Portrait of a Parisian Woman, 1867
charcoal 22×14¼ in.
Brussels, Bibliothèque Royale

JAKOB MARIS   Canal with a Bridge   *black chalk* $7\frac{1}{2} \times 9\frac{3}{4}$ *in.*
Otterlo, Holland, Rijksmuseum Kröller-Müller

ANTON MAUVE Little Pine Wood *black chalk* $8\frac{1}{2} \times 11\frac{1}{4}$ *in.*
Otterlo, Holland, Rijksmuseum Kröller-Müller

SUZE ROBERTSON Seated Girl   *charcoal*   *19¾ × 12¾ in.*
The Hague, Gemeentemuseum

VINCENT VAN GOGH The Gleaner, about 1885   *black chalk*   *20¼ × 16¼ in.*
Essen, Germany, Museum Folkwang

VINCENT VAN GOGH Cypresses, 1889   *reed pen with black chalk on colored paper   12¼ × 9 in.*
Otterlo, Holland, Rijksmuseum Kröller-Müller

CONSTANTIN MEUNIER The Return of the Miners, about 1895 *chalk and charcoal* $35 \times 52\frac{3}{8}$ *in.*
Ixelles, Brussels, Musée Constantin Meunier

JAMES ENSOR Masquerade with a Skeleton   *crayon* $9\frac{3}{4} \times 13\frac{1}{2}$ *in.*
Brussels, Bibliothèque Royale

JAMES ENSOR Self-portrait, 1885 *crayon* $8\frac{1}{2} \times 6\frac{3}{4}$ *in.*
Brussels, collection M. Mabille

JAKOB SMITS Mother and Child *charcoal* $9 \times 7\frac{3}{4}$ *in.*
Brussels, Bibliothèque Royale

GEORGES MINNE The Weeping Mother, 1890   *crayon   15¼ × 11¼ in.*
Sauvagemont-Couture St-Germain, Brussels, collection Jules van Paemel

JAN TOOROP The Three Brides, 1893 *colored chalk and crayon* *30¾ × 38½ in.*
Otterlo, Holland, Rijksmuseum Kröller-Müller

FERNAND KHNOPFF Head of a Woman *pastel* $6\frac{3}{4} \times 5$ *in.*
Brussels, Bibliothèque Royale

253

JOSEPH ISRAELS Woman Drinking Coffee, about 1905 *black chalk 10¾ × 15 in.*
Otterlo, Holland, Rijksmuseum Kröller-Müller

ISAAC ISRAELS Young Woman, 1894   *black chalk*   *18½ × 16½ in.*
Otterlo, Holland, Rijksmuseum Kröller-Müller

255

HENRI JACQUES ÉDOUARD EVENEPOEL Standing Woman
charcoal $7\frac{3}{4} \times 4\frac{1}{4}$ *in.*
Brussels, Bibliothèque Royale

Sculpture

ANONYMOUS The Apostles St. Matthew, St. Andrew, and St. Bartholomew, about 1480 *stone height 24 in.*
Halle, Belgium, St. Martin

CLAUS SLUTER   Head of Christ: from The Calvary, 1399   *stone   height 24 in.*
Dijon, Chartreuse de Champmol

CLAUS SLUTER Moses (detail): from the Well of Moses,
1395-1404 *stone height 66¾ in.*
Dijon, Chartreuse de Champmol

CLAUS SLUTER Zacharias (detail): from the Well of Moses,
1395-1404 *stone height 70½ in.*
Dijon, Chartreuse de Champmol

ADRIAEN VAN WESEL Three Music-making Angels with Joseph, about 1477 *oak* $17\frac{1}{2} \times 14\frac{3}{4}$ *in.*
Amsterdam, Rijksmuseum

JAN BORMAN the ELDER
Altarpiece of St. George, 1493
oak 63 × 192¾ in.
Brussels, Musées Royaux d'Art et d'Histoire
a left wing
b right wing
c central panel

MASTER OF JOACHIM AND ANNA
The Meeting of Joachim and Anna, 1470-80   *oak   height 18¼ in.*
Amsterdam, Rijksmuseum

CONRAD MEYT Tomb of Margaret of Austria, 1531 *marble 228 × 137¾ in.*
Brou, France, St. Nicolas

JAN MONET Retable, 1533 *alabaster*
Halle, Belgium, St. Martin

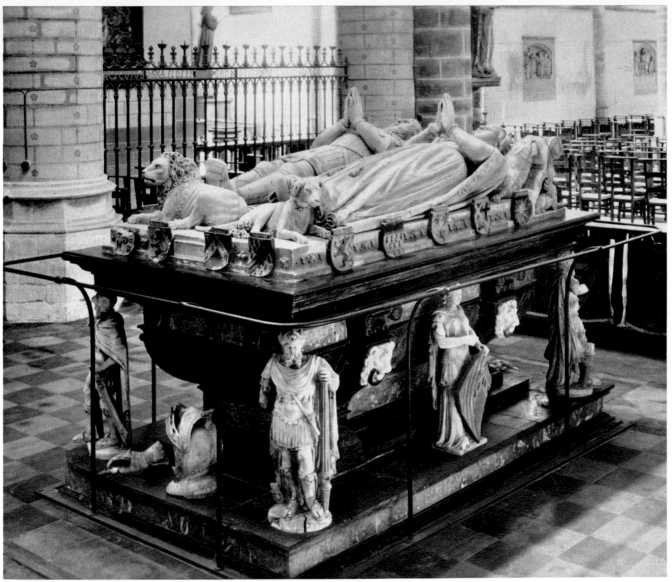

CORNELIS FLORIS Tomb of Jean III de Mérode and Anne de Ghistelle *marble*
Geel, Belgium, Ste. Dymphne

GIOVANNI DA BOLOGNA Astronomy
gilded bronze   height 24¼ in.
Vienna, Kunsthistorisches Museum

ADRIAEN DE VRIES A Seated Girl, 1600-25
lead height 16½ in.
London, Victoria and Albert Museum

HENDRIK DE KEYSER Reclining Figure of the Prince of Orange (detail): from the Tomb of William the Silent, Prince of Orange, about 1616 *marble   lifesize*
Delft, Nieuwe Kerk

Attributed to HENDRIK DE KEYSER Fortune: from the façade of a house in Amsterdam   *sandstone* $34\frac{1}{2} \times 32\frac{1}{4}$ *in.*
Amsterdam, Rijksmuseum

FRANS DUQUESNOY St. Andrew, 1633 *marble*
Rome, St. Peter's

ARTUS QUELLINUS the ELDER Atlas: figure surmounting the pediment, 1655
figure—*bronze   height of statue 252 in.*   globe—*brass   diameter 126 in.*   pedestal—*sandstone   height 49¼ in.*
Amsterdam, Town Hall

ARTUS QUELLINUS the ELDER St. Peter, 1658 *marble 89¾×37¼ in.*
Antwerp, St. André

ROMBOUT VERHULST Venus, about 1650 *marble 73¾ × 50 in.*
Amsterdam, Town Hall

ROMBOUT VERHULST
Tomb of Maria van Reygersberg and Willem van Lyere
1663   *marble*   137¾ × 63 *in.*
Katwijk, Holland, Reformed Church

GABRIEL GRUPELLO
Fountain for the Fishmongers' Guild, 1675
marble   height of upper part 34¼ in.
height of lower part 46¼ in.
Brussels, Musées Royaux des Beaux-Arts

MICHEL VERVOORT Pulpit, 1721 *wood*
Malines, Belgium, Cathedral

JOSEPH MENDES DA COSTA   Fish Vendors in Amsterdam, 1893   *terracotta* $8\frac{3}{4} \times 11\frac{1}{2}$ *in.*
The Hague, Gemeentemuseum

CONSTANTIN MEUNIER The Ironworker, 1886 *bronze height 57 in.*
Brussels, Musées Royaux des Beaux-Arts

CONSTANTIN MEUNIER   The Harvest: relief detail from the Monument to Labor, 1898   *stone* $94\frac{1}{2} \times 165\frac{1}{2}$ *in.*
Ixelles, Brussels, Musée Constantin Meunier

PAUL DE VIGNE   Portrait of Marnix van
St. Aldegonde   *bronze   height 18¼ in.*
Antwerp, Musée Royal des Beaux-Arts

KAREL VAN DER STAPPEN   The Sphinx, 1898
marble   height 28 in.
Brussels, Musées Royaux des Beaux-Arts

GEORGES MINNE   Kneeling Figure, 1896
marble $30\frac{3}{4} \times 12\frac{1}{4}$ *in.*
Ghent, Musée des Beaux-Arts

GEORGES MINNE
St. John the Baptist, 1895
stone 28 × 19¼ in.
Ghent, Musée des Beaux-Arts

GEORGES MINNE Solidarity, 1898 *bronze* *26¼ × 26¾ in.*
Brussels, Musées Royaux des Beaux-Arts

LAMBERTUS ZIJL Binding Corn (detail) 1917 *bronze* $16\frac{3}{4}$ *in.*
Otterlo, Holland, Rijksmuseum Kröller-Müller

LAMBERTUS ZIJL
Corner Figure of Gysbrecht van Amstel, 1903
sandstone $107\frac{1}{2} \times 28\frac{3}{4}$ *in.*
Amsterdam, The Exchange

Influences and Developments

Exterior of Notre Dame des Victoires   *Tournai*

Romanesque and Gothic Architecture in the Netherlands

Architecture was the dominant cultural expression of the Romanesque and Gothic period. Reflections, if not direct images, of the architectural outlook are to be found in most of the creative activity of the time. The major examples of religious architecture, found mainly in the southern part of the Netherlands, are therefore an essential background to an understanding of Flemish and Dutch art, not only in painting and sculpture, but also in murals, stained glass, and manuscript illustration.

The importance of French influence must not be overlooked; nevertheless, religious architecture in the Netherlands soon evolved its own particular local character. The Romanesque period is represented by a few buildings of great importance—Tournai (p. 286) and (a), Maastricht, and Rolduc. The Gothic cathedrals of Brussels (b) and 's Hertogenbosch (c) reflect something of the majesty of the earlier Gothic of northern France.

The true expression of the rich and proud middle class was, however, the small town typical of Flanders and Brabant, often with an important town hall, characteristic high tower (d), and guild houses. A high standard of craftsmanship rather than outstanding individual achievement was the basis of this civic and domestic architecture.

a Transept of Notre Dame des Victoires
Tournai

b Exterior of St. Michel (*formerly* St. Gudule)
Brussels

c Exterior of 's Hertogenbosch Cathedral
's Hertogenbosch

d The Belfry
Bruges

a

b

c

d

Painting and Illumination in the 15th Century

During the 15th century the artist was still dependent on the church or the court for patronage, though a growing sense of individuality was spreading throughout Europe. The court centers, particularly those of Burgundy, Bruges, and Ghent, were outstanding for their magnificence. This is reflected in the many manuscripts commissioned by the royal dukes, and it was in this art that the Flemish concern with realism first emerged.

Most of the art produced was of a religious nature. The illuminated manuscripts were occasionally chronicles of recent history, but more often they were prayer books or religious histories. Philip the Good is shown during the celebration of High Mass (a), and in this age it was normal to portray a donor or patron in a religious setting. Jan van Eyck was a court painter, but the greater part of his work was devoted to the representation of religious themes. The teaching of the church was still the predominant factor in society. The van Eycks' *Last Judgment* (d) and the anonymous *Apocalypse* (c) depict themes that were uppermost in the minds of people in the 15th century. The significance of life lay primarily in the teachings of the church; the growing humanist ideal had not yet challenged its power.

The development of Flemish art can be clearly traced in the evolution of illuminated manuscripts. Ducal patronage encouraged the depiction of secular as well as religious events. The calendar pages of the *Très Riches Heures*, painted for the Duke of Berri by the Limbourg brothers, represent a tremendous achievement in the earliest stages of landscape and genre painting. This interest in the realities of everyday life was continued by the brothers Jan and Hubert van Eyck, by Robert Campin, and by most of the northern painters who followed them.

a

b

c

d

The Treatment of Religious Themes

The treatment of religious themes became increasingly varied toward the end of the Middle Ages; each painting on this page represents a different approach to the subject.

The Madonna of Canon van der Paele (c) is a rich and hieratic picture. The figures are situated in the apse of a church and are wearing rich, jeweled garments. Although the Virgin is not idealized to any great extent, as she would have been in an Italian picture of a comparable date, she is nevertheless set above the other figures on a throne with steps leading up to it. Every object in the painting is decorated and the colors are polished and jewel-like. The scene is objectively treated and there is no sense of a deep personal religious emotion. The van der Paele altarpiece is an example of courtly art.

The panel after Roger van der Weyden (a) represents a very different approach. There is no ornamental background and the head and shoulders of the Virgin and Child fill the space of the painting. *St. Luke Painting the Virgin* by Roger van der Weyden (d) is different again. The composition is based quite closely on *The Madonna of the Chancellor Rolin* by Jan van Eyck, but van der Weyden's picture is simpler and more informal. The Virgin, the Child, and St. Luke are seated in a house and although the surroundings are rich, only the brocaded hanging behind the Virgin suggests that she is set apart from St. Luke. In the background there is a landscape and the tiny figures of people going about their daily life. The middle distance is filled by a walled garden in which two figures in contemporary dress are looking out toward the landscape.

Gerard David's *Madonna of the Milk Soup* (b) has a domestic setting. The atmosphere is homely and the close-up view of the mother feeding soup to her child has no implication of Mary as Queen of Heaven. The painter has added touches of interest in the two still-life groups and the landscape seen through a window. The softer, sentimental style of painting shows the influence of Quentin Massys, who in turn had been influenced by Italian art.

a After Roger van der Weyden
Madonna and Child, about 1454
oil on panel diameter 7 in.
Houston, Texas, Museum of Fine Arts

b Gerard David
The Madonna of the Milk Soup,
about 1520
oil on panel 14 × 11¼ in.
*Brussels, Musées Royaux des
Beaux-Arts*

c Jan van Eyck
The Madonna of Canon van der
Paele, 1436
oil on panel 48 × 62 in.
Bruges, Musée Communal

d Roger van der Weyden
St. Luke Painting the Virgin,
about 1440
oil on panel 54½ × 43½ in.
Munich, Alte Pinakothek

a

b

c

d

Sculpture in the 15th and 16th Centuries

During the 15th and 16th centuries there was a considerable interchange of ideas between painting and sculpture. Until the classical ideal took root in northern Europe, sculpture was usually colored. The intention was to make it as lifelike as possible and to blend it with the brightly colored surroundings of the churches. Often sculpture and painting were combined in the same altarpiece.

The altarpiece carved by Jan Borman the Elder in 1493 (b) is very realistic in the details of its figures and architecture. It was planned to look like a tableau or painting. It was also customary to decorate the outer wings of an altarpiece with figures of saints painted in monochrome and apparently placed in niches. These paintings not only resembled sculpture in their coloring but also in the full and heavy treatment of the form (a).

There was a close association between figures and their architectural settings (d, e). This is true of the carvings in tympanums of Romanesque churches, of carved altarpieces and those decorated by paintings. Originally the sculptures were inseparable not only from their immediate background but also from the construction of the church as a whole. From this tradition of northern sculpture emerged the interest in the representation of spatial values and the third dimension.

a

b

c

c Claus Sluter
Mourner: from the Tomb of Philip
the Bold, about 1404
alabaster
Dijon, Musée des Beaux-Arts

d Anonymous
The Virgin, from the south portal
Halle, Belgium, St. Martin

e Attributed to Jan Borman the Elder
St. John   *oak*
Louvain, St. Pierre

d

e

Hieronymus Bosch and the Changing Spirit of the 15th Century

Before the Italian Renaissance style was fully integrated with the Flemish idiom, Hieronymus Bosch was painting in a manner distinct from local 15th-century tradition. His work combines the waning mysticism and symbolism of the Middle Ages, as seen in *Hell: from the Pilgrimage of Human Life* (c), and the questing spirit of the Renaissance. Fantastic figures posture in the characteristic gestures of Romanesque sculpture (a, b). Bosch's idiosyncratic symbolism is difficult to interpret, but his images are based on familiar, closely observed objects and animals. The innovations of Bosch's paintings, his insight, naturalism, and a feeling for light and space reminiscent of the van Eycks, anticipate 16th-century painting. Pieter Bruegel is his natural successor. Bosch's symbolism and fantasy look ahead to the imagery of James Ensor, four centuries later, and the terrible phantoms of surrealism.

a The Fall of Simon the Magician
Autun, France, St. Lazare

b The Weighing of Souls,
from the tympanum
Autun, France, St. Lazare

c Hell: from the Pilgrimage of
Human Life (manuscript)
Brussels, Musées Royaux des Beaux-Arts

d Hieronymus Bosch
The Temptation of St. Anthony
(detail) about 1500
Lisbon, Museu Nacional de Arte Antiga

a

b

c

d

Italy and the Netherlands in the 15th Century

The key development in both northern and Italian art in the 15th century was a closer representation of reality. In Italy Brunelleschi had evolved a scientific method of perspective that enabled the artist to give an illusion of space and depth. This technique was unknown in northern Europe until the time of Dürer, who was the main conductor of Renaissance ideas to the North. The painters of Flanders achieved their realism by an accumulation of detail. Each culture, however, began to affect the other.

With Masaccio's fresco *St. Peter's Shadow Healing the Sick* (a) the spectator for the first time faces a completely articulated world in which light is the unifying factor. The paintings of Jan van Eyck are also governed by the subtleties of light. The *Portrait of Giovanni Arnolfini* (d) is bathed in a sensitively observed light, and the structural forms are evident beneath the detailed painting of the features.

Flemish painting was greatly admired by many Italians, but Antonello da Messina (b) was the only Italian painter to be radically influenced by the minute oil technique practiced in the Netherlands. His *St. Jerome in his Study*, National Gallery, London, may be derived from part of a van Eyck triptych known to have been in Naples in 1456. Several of Roger van der Weyden's paintings show elements that reflect the work of artists such as Fra Angelico. Piero della Francesca shows certain similarities to Flemish art in his handling of detail. His *Portrait of Federico da Montefeltro* (c) has a realism parallel to that of van Eyck, and the landscape background is reminiscent of Hans Memling.

Flemish technique influenced Venetian painting and the portraits executed by Giovanni Bellini, in particular, have traces of a Flemish type of design. Even Leonardo da Vinci's *Portrait of Ginevra de' Benci* suggests that he had studied the subtle transitions in the landscape of Hugo van der Goes' *Portinari Altarpiece*.

a

a Masaccio
St. Peter's Shadow Healing the Sick
fresco
Florence, S. Maria del Carmine,
Brancacci Chapel

b Antonello da Messina
The Crucifixion, 1475
oil on panel 21 × 16¼ in.
Antwerp, Musée Royal des Beaux-Arts

c Piero della Francesca
Portrait of Federico da Montefeltro,
about 1466
oil on panel 18½ × 13 in.
Florence, Uffizi

d Jan van Eyck
Portrait of Giovanni Arnolfini
oil on panel 11½ × 8 in.
West Berlin, Staatliche Museen

b

c

d

The 16th Century—Pieter Bruegel the Elder

Pieter Bruegel the Elder traveled to Italy in about 1552. A drawing of Reggio in flames, when the town was sacked by the Turks in 1552, indicates that he journeyed south that year, probably also to Messina. He was in Rome in 1553 and the next year he returned over the Alps, where he made numerous landscape drawings.

Although Bruegel's work seems to be typically Flemish there are elements in his style of the Mannerist convention: his frequent use of the panoramic viewpoint and the composite landscape; the overlong proportions and exaggerated attitudes that appear in some of his paintings; his concern with movement into space. These characteristics of Mannerism stem from his visit to Italy and his contact with the Brussels romanists.

Bruegel certainly learned much from Venetian art. His treatment of landscape was influenced by artists such as Titian, and many of his rustic scenes show similarities to the paintings of Jacopo Bassano (d). Bruegel's influence on Tintoretto can be seen by comparing (b) and (c). Clear similarities are the dramatic, shortened forms, the steep perspective, and the array of crowded figures. His interest in composition led Bruegel to experiment with many forms and viewpoints, and some of these can be seen in *The Harvesters* (e) and *The Land of Cockayne* (a).

The dominant element in Bruegel's art is the richness of the manner in which he continues the traditions of Flemish realism. His feeling for texture and surface, and his interest in every aspect of nature and life, not only carry on the Eyckian traditions but anticipate the 17th century.

a

a Pieter Bruegel the Elder
The Land of Cockayne, 1567
oil on panel 20¼ × 31 in.
Munich, Alte Pinakothek

b Pieter Bruegel the Elder
The Peasant Wedding, about 1568
oil on panel 45 × 64¼ in.
Vienna, Kunsthistorisches Museum

c Jacopo Tintoretto
The Last Supper, 1592-94
oil on canvas 144 × 223¼ in.
Venice, S. Giorgio Maggiore

d Jacopo Bassano
The Grape Harvesters
Rome, Galleria Doria

e Pieter Bruegel the Elder
The Harvesters, 1565
oil on panel 46¼ × 63 in.
New York, Metropolitan Museum of Art

b

c

d

e

Some Themes of 17th-Century Painting

In the 17th century artists explored many new kinds of subject matter. The church and the aristocracy were no longer the only patrons; the rich middle classes also wanted paintings to hang in their homes, and to commemorate their guilds and societies.

Portraiture gained steadily in importance. Sir Anthony van Dyck, whose work consisted mainly of portraits, was granted a title by Charles I of England and pursued a successful career. On a more modest level painters such as Cornelis de Vos (d) and Bartholomeus van der Helst (e) recorded the appearance of their contemporaries.

For the first time landscape (b, c) and still-life (a) were considered worthy subjects in their own right and were no longer used merely in a subordinate role. Flemish and Dutch painters delighted in portraying flowers and fruit in a richly detailed, illusionistic style.

a

b

a Osias Beert
A Vase of Flowers, about 1620
oil on panel 24 × 18 in.
Oxford, Ashmolean Museum

b Rubens
Landscape, about 1636
oil on panel 19½ × 21¼ in.
Rotterdam, Boymans-van Beuningen Museum

c Philips de Koninck
Landscape
oil on canvas 52¼ × 65 in.
Munich, Alte Pinakothek

d Cornelis de Vos
The Painter with his Family, 1621
oil on canvas 74 × 64 in.
Brussels, Musées Royaux des Beaux-Arts

e Bartholomeus van der Helst
Portrait of Gerard Bicker,
Bailiff of Muiden
oil on panel 37 × 27¾ in.
Amsterdam, Rijksmuseum

c

d

e

Interiors and Genre Painting of the 17th Century

The Counter Reformation tended to encourage a new humanism. The church sponsored an art that created an accessible image of the beyond, and made an appeal to the senses and emotions. The devotion to the saints widened the subject range covered by religious art and many new styles and methods of painting were introduced. Splendid cathedrals and churches were built, and many altarpieces were commissioned.

Caravaggio was the outstanding and most influential painter of the era in Italy. He revolted against the classicizing, idealized art of the Carracci, and gave a new life to painting by turning to the material of everyday life. The models for Caravaggio's works were the humblest types of his contemporaries. On his canvases they became the saints and heroes of religious narrative. This led to a secularization of the subject without, however, losing the inherent transcendental quality. Caravaggio constructed his paintings with great simplicity, and introduced violent contrasts of light and shadow, combined with a wealth of detail. His directness, his depiction of real life, and above all his dramatic lighting effects made a great impact (a). Painters such as Hendrick Terbrugghen (b), Theodor Rombouts (c), Adriaen Brouwer (d), and Gerard van Honthorst, spread Caravaggio's style into France (e) and all over Europe. Caravaggio influenced Velázquez and Rubens and paved the way for Rembrandt and even Jan Vermeer.

a

b

c

d

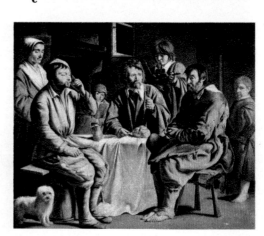

e

The Reformation and the Counter Reformation—Architecture

The Protestant North, after gaining its independence from Spain in 1581, tended to favor a more sober art and architectural style than that followed in the Southern Netherlands. The devout merchants of Holland never accepted the full Baroque style, which was more in keeping with the exuberance of the southern manner. The differences of taste were more sharply perceptible in architecture than in painting.

Church architecture in the Protestant areas made a complete break with the Catholic atmosphere of the southern states. It tended toward a classicism grafted onto a Gothic tradition. Secular architecture also tended toward classicism, carrying on the forms that had been established during the Renaissance. Jacob van Campen, who designed the Town Hall in Amsterdam (a, b), had visited Italy. In this building his simplicity and feeling for space achieved great dignity.

The Jesuit Church of St. Charles Borromeo in Antwerp was designed by the architect Pieter Huyssens and built between 1615 and 1621. It followed the ground plan of the traditional Brussels church but introduced typically Baroque elements in the elevation and the vaulting. The church was burned down in 1718 and the Baroque decorations were omitted when it was rebuilt (d, e). Originally the interior was richly decorated with designs by Rubens.

Rubens' house, also in Antwerp, probably influenced the design of St. Charles Borromeo and other churches. It must have been begun soon after 1610 and was probably completed seven years later. Rubens was interested in architecture and his house shows a mixture of Mannerism and Baroque in the design and details (c).

a Jacob van Campen
Exterior of the Town Hall, 1655
Amsterdam

b Jacob van Campen
Gallery of the Town Hall, 1655
Amsterdam

c Rubens
Exterior of Rubens' House
Antwerp

d Pieter Huyssens
Interior of St. Charles Borromeo
1615-21
Antwerp

e Pieter Huyssens
Exterior of St. Charles Borromeo
1615-21
Antwerp

a

b

c

d

e

The Double Portrait

a Rubens
Helena Fourment with her Son
oil on panel 57½ × 40 *in.*
Munich, Alte Pinakothek

b Rembrandt
The Artist with Saskia, about 1634
oil on canvas 63¼ × 52 *in.*
Dresden, Gemäldegalerie

The work of Rubens and Rembrandt reflects the politico-cultural division of the Low Countries in the 17th century. Rubens worked in the international environment of the Spanish Netherlands, and Rembrandt in the cultivated mercantile milieu of the Dutch republic in the north. Rubens lived the life of a cosmopolitan diplomat whereas much of Rembrandt's energy was consumed by his life-long struggle to maintain his artistic integrity and financial status.

Rubens, by virtue of his wide travels and contact with the courts of Mantua, Spain, and Paris, developed an exuberance in subject matter and technique that ranks him among the greatest names of northern Baroque art. Rembrandt, on the other hand, executed many of his most intense religious engravings and portraits of deep psychological awareness in the far humbler, more intimate environment of the Jewish quarter in Amsterdam. This difference of approach manifests itself in a contrasting treatment of similar themes.

a

b

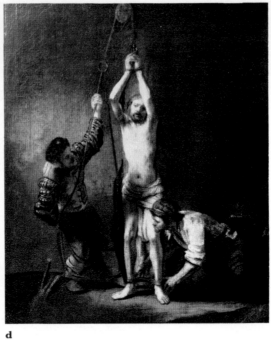

The Treatment of
Biblical Themes

c Rubens
The Crucifixion, 1620
oil on panel   169 × 122¼ in.
Antwerp, Musée Royal des Beaux-Arts

d Rembrandt
The Flagellation, 1658
oil on canvas   36½ × 28½ in.
Darmstadt, Hessisches Landesmuseum

The Treatment
of Mythological Themes

e Rubens
The Abduction of the Daughters
of Leucippus, 1616
oil on canvas   87½ × 82 in.
Munich, Alte Pinakothek

f Rembrandt
The Abduction of Ganymede, 1635
oil on canvas   67½ × 51 in.
Dresden, Gemäldegalerie

c

d

e

f

299

a

b

The Portrait and Society

Until the spread of humanism made portraiture an acceptable aesthetic subject, depiction of actual personages had been limited to idealized donor figures in religious paintings, and kings and princes in illuminated manuscripts and missals. However, in sepulchral and monumental sculpture portraits had been employed more frequently. During and immediately after the Renaissance various facets of the portrait painter's duty emerged. The problem was to achieve a satisfactory compromise between truth to reality, the flattery required to satisfy the patron, an impression of the sitter's power and position, and the personal interpretation of the artist.

A strong interest in portraiture developed in northern Europe in the 15th century; Flemish painters became particularly interested in textures and surfaces. A keen and uncompromising observation is displayed by the portrait of Maria Portinari from Hugo van der Goes' *Portinari Altarpiece* (a). *The Portrait of a Prelate* (c), about 1476, attributed to Cornelis van Cleve, the guild portraits, and the paintings of van Dyck, reveal different aspects of portraiture in the 16th and 17th centuries. Family groups and guild groups became especially popular with the rise of a prosperous middle class in the 17th century.

Sir Anthony van Dyck, working mainly at the English court, pursued a successful career as a portrait painter. The delicacy of his palette, his feeling for the silks and satins worn by his sitters, and above all his sense of the melancholy elegance to which the fashionable aspired, helped to create the accepted image of the society for which he worked (d). He set the pattern of portraiture throughout Europe for the next two centuries.

a Hugo van der Goes
Maria Portinari (detail): from the
Portinari Altarpiece, about 1476
Florence, Uffizi

b Lucas van Leyden
Portrait of a Lady
*Rotterdam, Museum
Boymans-van Beuningen*

c Cornelis van Cleve
Portrait of a Prelate, about 1476
*oil on panel $28\frac{1}{4} \times 21\frac{3}{4}$ in.
Moreton-in-Marsh, England,
collection Capt. E. G. Spencer Churchill*

d Sir Anthony van Dyck
Portrait of Lord John and
Lord Bernard Stuart, 1638
*oil on canvas 95×58 in.
Romsey, England, collection the late
Countess Mountbatten of Burma*

c

d

Landscape Painting in the 19th Century

Landscape painting in the 19th century was radically affected by the work of Constable and Turner. Constable had a profound influence on Eugène Delacroix and French Romantic art, the Barbizon School, and the Impressionists, and Turner particularly influenced the Impressionists. Constable and Turner represent two peaks of the Romantic movement in art, whose dominant characteristic was an interest in landscape painting for its own sake.

Constable's work (c) owes much to earlier English Romantics such as Richard Wilson, but also to his understanding of the European landscape tradition, particularly 17th-century Dutch landscapes. Much of his feeling for moving light and shadow was derived from Jakob van Ruisdael.

Turner's work developed from an Italianate style of classical landscape to a freer and more romantic vision. To what extent he influenced Impressionism is hard to estimate. In vision and technique he certainly anticipated the most extreme Impressionist phase of Manet, and Claude Monet and Camille Pissarro are known to have admired his paintings on their visit to England in 1871. The Dutch painter Johan Barthold Jongkind was also working at this time in a manner that looked forward to Monet and the Impressionists.

The Barbizon School, whose chief members were Millet, Théodore Rousseau (d), and Diaz de la Peña, did not altogether push aside tradition. It had a considerable influence throughout Europe; echoes of it are found in the paintings of Joseph Israels and the Hague School, and in the work of Hippolyte Boulenger (a, b) and the school of Tervueren, although these artists owed most to their Dutch forerunners. Boulenger was the most notable painter of his group and his style is at times close to that of Corot.

a

b

c

d

e

a Hippolyte Boulenger
Spring at Boîtsfort
Tournai, Musée

b Hippolyte Boulenger
L'avenue des Charmes à Tervueren
1871
oil on canvas   51¼ × 37 in.
Brussels, Musées Royaux des Beaux-Arts

c John Constable
The Hay-Wain, 1821
oil on canvas   51 × 73 in.
London, National Gallery

d Théodore Rousseau
A Group of Oak Trees, Apremont
Paris, Louvre

e Jakob Maris
A Ship on a Beach, 1878
oil on canvas   49 × 41¼ in.
The Hague, Gemeentemuseum

The Theme of "Labor"

During the 19th century many artists were aware of existing social problems. The theme of peasants and laborers occurs frequently. The summit of this expression of social consciousness is reached in the work of Vincent van Gogh, but a background to his painting can be traced in most of the European countries.

Van Gogh much admired the work of Millet (b). His own religious feelings were in sympathy with Millet's work, and he shared the vision of the peasants' toil as something mighty and grand. In fact, van Gogh was less given to pathos than Millet, and was closer to nature. The desire to depict the laborer's toil was strengthened by his life among the peasants, and by reading the works of the French writer Émile Zola. For van Gogh the life of the weavers and miners was particularly significant and he made many paintings and drawings of them (d).

a Gustave Courbet
The Stonebreakers, 1850
oil on canvas   62¾ × 102 in.
(*destroyed* World War II)
formerly Dresden, Gemäldegalerie

b Jean François Millet
The Wood Carriers, about 1874
oil on canvas   31 × 38½ in.
Cardiff, National Gallery of Wales

c Charles de Groux
The Blessing
oil on canvas   16 × 31 in.
Ghent, Musée des Beaux-Arts

a

b

c

In France the outstanding painter of the laborer's life was Courbet (a). His interest in politics, and his connections with socialism, gave his work a particular character. In contrast to the devout Millet, he was violently anti-clerical. A parallel feeling for the problems of the worker existed in Belgium. In his *Monument to Labor* (f) the painter and sculptor Constantin Meunier expressed in plastic terms his feeling for the dignity of labor and sympathy for the laborer, and this heroic image was carried out in a style reminiscent of Donatello and Auguste Rodin.

Charles de Groux was closest to Millet in his treatment of social themes (c), but his work was marred by sentimentality. Some foretaste of Expressionism is found in the paintings of Laermans (e), whose compositions are both weighty and rhythmical, and have similarities with Gauguin's paintings of Brittany. The mixture of social sentiment and "primitive" earthy form, gives a poignancy to Laermans' work.

d Vincent van Gogh
Interior with Weaver, 1884
oil on canvas   24 × 37 in.
Otterlo, Rijksmuseum Kröller-Müller

e Eugène Laermans
Death, 1904
oil on canvas   47¾ × 69 in.
Brussels, Musées Royaux des Beaux-Arts

f Constantin Meunier
Industry: from the Monument to Labor
stone
Brussels, Parc du Cinquantenaire

d

e

f

James Ensor and the Post-Impressionist Generation

The work of James Ensor developed from Realism and Impressionism. His early works are reminiscent of Manet, and of the Belgian, Guillaume Vogels. Ensor painted in Ostend on the Belgian coast, and until about 1883 was concerned mainly with the light and color in which to express everyday life. In January, 1884, Ensor and Théodore van Rysselberghe were among the founders of an avant garde art society in Brussels—Les XX. The most stimulating painters of the time, including van Gogh and Cézanne, were invited to exhibit with them.

Ensor's style changed in 1883, when he painted *The Scandalized Masks*. From this time an element of fantasy was present in his work, and he used masks and skeletons to make a comment on the undercurrents of human life. The introduction of the theme of masks was of great importance, for it left Ensor at liberty to distort freely for effect, and made him one of the forerunners of Expressionism.

From 1887, after the exhibition of work by Georges Seurat with Les XX, Ensor's palette lightened, but his subject matter became more biting. His huge painting of *The Entry of Christ into Brussels in 1889* (e), was refused even by Les XX. His color is light and rich, often applied in small strokes, but has none of the calm quality apparent in the luminist work of Claus (b) and in the divisionist paintings of Théodore van Rysselberghe (d), who followed the examples of Seurat and Signac, and explored the scientific theories of color.

Ensor remained a solitary figure, and it was many years before his paintings were appreciated. After about 1890 his work became repetitive and less powerful, but the best of it drew the attention of many painters, among them Paul Klee and Marc Chagall, and the German, Emil Nolde, and helped to shape the development of both Expressionism and Surrealism.

a James Ensor
   La Femme au Nez Retroussé, 1879
   oil on canvas 21½ × 18 in.
   Antwerp, Musée Royal des Beaux-Arts

b Émile Claus
   Summer, 1893
   oil on canvas 23 × 36 in.
   Antwerp, Musée Royal des Beaux-Arts

c James Ensor
   Studio Utensils
   oil on canvas 32½ × 44½ in.
   Munich, Neue Pinakothek

d Théodore van Rysselberghe
   A Family Gardening, 1890
   oil on canvas 45½ × 64 in.
   Otterlo, Rijksmuseum Kröller-Müller

e James Ensor
   The Entry of Christ into Brussels
   in 1889, 1888
   oil on canvas 98½ × 171 in.
   Antwerp, Musée Royal des Beaux-Arts,
   lent by Mrs. Louis Franck, London

a

b

c

d

e

THE VOLUMES

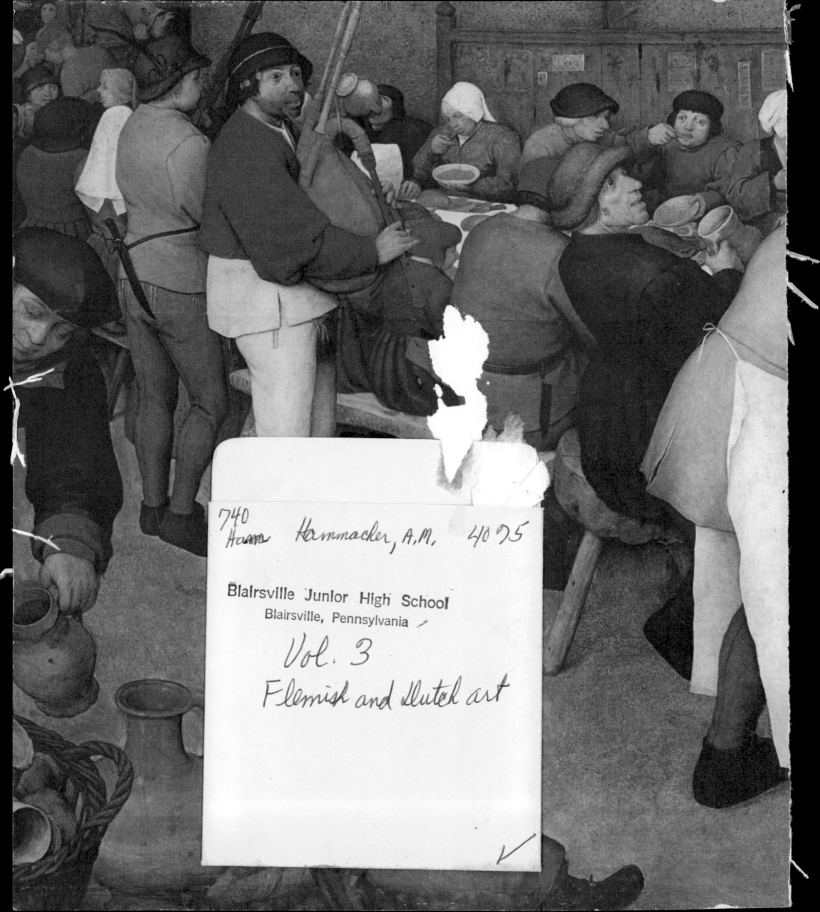